HEIRLOOMS in NEEDLEPOINT

For Hannah and Jo

HEIRLOOMS in NEEDLEPOINT

50 Classic Original Designs

Sue Hawkins

NEW HOLLAND

ACKNOWLEDGEMENTS

My thanks go firstly to my family: John, Hannah and Jo who helped whenever possible, put up with the disruptions at home and did not complain (too much). Then to Munni Srivastava whose enthusiasm for my work made me believe this book was possible. To the ladies who stitched and without whom I could never have finished it all: Jenny Jackson, Kathy Elliott, Olive McAnerney, Caroline Gibbons, Eileen Blackeby, Liz Cook and Alwyn Peters. To Nina Ziegler for the loan of the family silver, even though it needed cleaning. Lastly and especially, to my good friend, Jane Greenoff, without whose help and encouragement I would still be sitting happily in the garden!

Thanks are also due to the following for loaning us materials and artefacts for photography: Decorative Textiles, 7 Suffolk Parade, Cheltenham, Gloucestershire GL50 2AB; Appleton Bros., Ltd, Thames Works, Church Street, Chiswick, London W4 2PE; Sudeley Castle, Winchcombe, Gloucestershire GL54 5JD.

This edition first published in 1997 by
New Holland (Publishers) Ltd

First published in 1994
by New Holland (Publishers) Ltd
London • Cape Town • Sydney • Singapore

24 Nutford Place
London W1H 6DQ
United Kingdom

80 McKenzie Street
Cape Town 8001
South Africa

3/2 Aquatic Drive
Frenchs Forest, NSW 2086
Australia

Copyright © Sue Hawkins, 1994
Copyright © Savitri Books (design & layout), 1994

A CIP catalogue record for this book is available from the British Library

ISBN 1 85368 618 2 (pb)

This book was conceived and produced by
Savitri Books Ltd
115J Cleveland Street
London W1P 5PN

Art direction and design by Mrinalini Srivastava

Edited by Caroline Taggart
Photography by Matthew Chattle
Typeset in Melior by Dorchester Typesetting Group Ltd
Printed in Singapore by Tien Wah Press (Pte) Ltd

CONTENTS

INTRODUCTION

My interest in needlepoint goes back a long way. Many years ago I used to work for an antique dealer, restoring old and treasured textiles. Later on, I came to run my own needlecraft shop and to produce kits from some of my original needlepoint designs.

Since then, I have to admit that I have become completely and unashamedly addicted to my needle and am rarely found without wools and canvas secreted somewhere about my person. I am often asked how I manage to produce fairly large pieces of work in a relatively short time. I think the underlying principle is that I love doing it. I cannot explain the feeling of contentment and peace I experience as I begin to stitch – the soothing, repetitive action has a strong calming effect. My other 'secret' is never to be without a piece of work handy. In this way, I can and do make use of any odd moment. My children seem to find it entertaining to see me sewing as I wait for a pan to come to the boil!

I find needlepoint a most rewarding technique, well suited to the bold patterns that attract me. The inspiration behind the projects contained in this book has come from antique and traditional design. It was strongly influenced by oriental rugs and carpets. The repeat geometric patterns almost 'urge' me on and I find it very difficult to tear myself away and want to finish one more repeat, turn the corner, finish the motif, start on the border... Traditional rug patterns are timeless. They complement most interiors – traditional or modern. They appeal to men as well as to women: this is a valid point now that increasing numbers of men have discovered the therapeutic effects of needlepoint.

The rich colours of oriental textiles and of Islamic ceramics are a challenge – it is not always easy to find yarn which will recreate the subtle shades as well as the depth of colour I wish to emulate. Yet the result is well worth the extra effort.

I am also much influenced by European traditional patterns such as bargello – flame stitch. To me it is like painting with a needle. I prefer the free-hand type of bargello in which the pattern runs randomly across the canvas, following, it seems, its own momentum. Crewel embroidery, which I first discovered in my textile-restoration days, is a favourite of mine. I mix it with needlepoint to produce a three-dimensional effect. It is an easy technique to master but requires a good eye to ensure successful shading of the colours.

All the projects in this book are based on counted-thread work. Some of the charts use symbols only, others use a combination of hand-coloured sections for large background areas and of symbols for the intricate motifs. If you have been used to working on printed canvas and have not tried counting from a chart, be prepared to have a go. It is infinitely more rewarding as you watch the lovely pattern grow on the blank canvas. Once you have mastered the technique – each small square on the chart represents one stitch on the canvas – you will probably never want to buy a printed canvas again. Do remember, however, that the majority of the patterns used in this book are, to a greater or lesser extent, geometric. A couple of extra stitches can throw the whole design out of kilter – corner patterns especially. Be strict with yourself and unpick as soon as you detect an error. It is a good idea to check from time to time that the pattern is correct and that no stitch or detail of the design has been missed.

As mentioned above, some projects involve some simple crewel embroidery. Do not be put off if you haven't done it before. There are detailed instructions on transferring the design onto canvas and on how to work the embroidery. Especially when worked in wool, it is a very 'forgiving' form of embroidery. Imagine that your needle is a brush and think of the long-and-short stitches as brush strokes. The shading and blending of the colours are very rewarding.

I would like to add a word about yarns. A quick look through this book and the yarn requirements specified for each project will show you that Appleton's crewel wools are one of my favourite embroidery yarns. I like their texture and the shades in which they are manufactured. At the back of this book you will find a conversion chart to DMC Médicis

wools for the colours I have used here. This is an excellent yarn too, but remember that the conversion chart will give only you the nearest available shade to the one I have used and that small differences in the final result are bound to take place. Throughout the book you will find Colour Guides. These colour bars show you what the colours specified look like. You can then decide to replace Appleton's wools by a different yarn and still keep more or less to the original colour scheme. Do not be afraid to experiment and to alter the colour scheme to suit your taste and requirements.

I am well aware how little free time most of us have and each range of projects also includes a variety of small gift items which can be completed in a few hours, yet will look stylish and distinctive. When you have completed the piece of embroidery of your choice, turn to the back of the book where you will find instructions on stretching and starching, and making-up techniques.

Finally, I would like to say that I have enjoyed immensely designing and working this collection of projects and I hope that you will derive as much pleasure from them as I did.

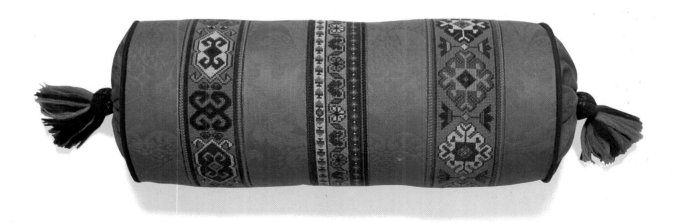

THE TUDOR COLLECTION

Tudor embroidery has always fascinated me with its bold and yet delicate floral motifs flowing freely over the cloth. The basic idea used in the two cushions and the fire screen came from a small seventeenth-century pillow worked in tent stitch, using silk thread on a very fine canvas. In my own design the flowers and the leaves are worked in long-and-short stitch – a method which ensures delicate shading and also makes the flowers stand out in relief over the smooth tent-stitch background. A border was called for and I decided that bargello would provide an attractive contrast.

Seventeenth-century pillow worked in tent stitch, using metal thread.

Large cushion with all-over embroidery. Overall size of cushion: 39 x 43 cm (15½ x 17 in). The same piece of embroidery was also mounted as a fire screen on the left.

Cushions and accessories with
Tudor-inspired motifs.

LARGE DESIGN FOR CUSHION OR FIRE SCREEN

- **You will need** *a 50 cm (20 in) square of size 14 interlock mono canvas*
- *Appleton's crewel wool in the shades and quantities given on page 11*
- *a waterproof medium-thickness felt-tipped pen*
- *1 needle size 22*
- *embroidery frame*

The same piece of embroidery can be made up as a large pipe-edged cushion or as a fire screen as shown on page 8. The drawing on the opposite page is a quarter of the finished size of the design. Enlarge it to the required size.

Place the enlarged drawing on a flat surface and secure it with masking tape. Centre the canvas over the drawing and secure it in the same way. The holes in the canvas will allow you to see the design clearly. Use the felt-tipped pen to trace the design on the canvas. Do not press too hard as the pen would go through the weave of the canvas rather than producing the smooth line that is required. Do not draw the broken line at the edge of the design which represents the beginning of the border. This line is there as a **guideline** only and you will need to count the threads on the canvas to ensure that you have the correct number on each side before you start working the border. This is vital if the bargello pattern is to work. The sketch shown below gives you the exact thread count.

Mount the marked canvas on the frame. Always work long-and-short stitch embroidery on a frame to keep the tension constant.

The embroidery is worked in the following order: the drawing on the canvas, the counted-thread insects, if and wherever desired (see charts and yarn requirements on page 13), the bargello border, *The yarn requirements opposite refer to the large design (cushion **or** fire screen) and the small design being the velvet cushion on page 15.*

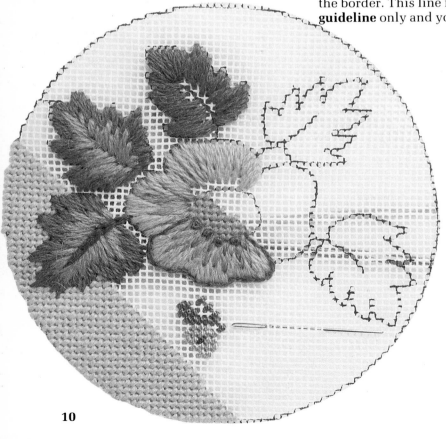

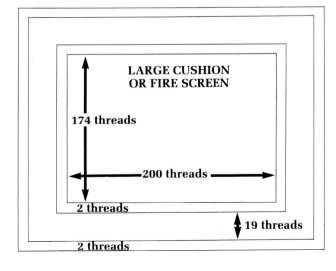

LARGE CUSHION OR FIRE SCREEN

174 threads

200 threads

2 threads

19 threads

2 threads

guideline only

172 threads

200 threads (see instructions for borders)

YARN REQUIREMENTS – Appleton's crewel wool

		large design page 8	small design page 15			large design page 8	small design page 15			large design page 8	small design page 15
	332	1 hank	2 skeins		695	3 skeins	2 skeins		204	2 skeins	1 skein
	334	2 hanks	4 skeins		154	3 skeins	2 skeins		205	4 skeins	2 skeins
	336	1 hank	2 skeins		156	3 skeins	2 skeins		207	1 skein	1 skein
	692	3 hanks	3 skeins		158	3 skeins	1 skein		932	2 skeins	1 skein
	693	2 skeins	1 skein		203	3 skeins	2 skeins		934	4 skeins	2 skeins

The main drawing. The flowers, the leaves, birds and stems are all worked using **three strands** of Appleton's crewel wool, except for the dark pink outline to the flowers which uses **one strand**.

Leaves. Begin with a spray close to the edge and work in long-and-short stitch (*see* page 110). Work from the outside towards the inside of the leaf (*see* the unfinished detail on page 10 which shows this clearly). The first layer of stitches is worked in 334. Work into every canvas hole around the leaf by overlapping in the centre. These first stitches may seem long but remember that the next layer is made into them.

The second layer of stitches (*see* unfinished detail again) is worked in the lighter green (332). The stitches radiate from the centre of the leaf outward, ensuring that each new stitch actually splits one of the darker existing ones.

The trunk of the tree and **the branches** are all worked in split back stitch (*see* page 109), using

number 336. Begin from the lower part of the trunk and work your way upwards.

Flowers and buds. These are worked using the three shades of pink: 203, 204 and 205 in that order. These three shades are used on all the petals except for those of the full rose on the left of the design (refer to the photograph of the cushion on page 8). In this rose I have used the 203 and 204 pinks and worked the turned-over edges and the small central petals in 205. The shading of the petals is worked in exactly the same way as the leaves, applying one layer of colour after another. The flowers are outlined in 207.

Small leaves, bases of flowers and buds. These are worked mostly in 334 with veins in 332 and calyxes in 336. The centres of the two open roses are worked in tent stitch (*see* page 109), using number 695. Fill these in **after** completing the petals and finish off by working a row of French knots (*see* page 109) in **three strands** of 932, carefully positioned so

that they sit on the intersection of the tent stitch and the long and short stitches.

The strawberries. These are worked in tent stitch, using 207 with tiny French knots worked in **one strand** of 695.

Bird on the left. The chest is worked in 205, the body in 204 and the wing in 932 (all in long-and-short stitch). The outline to the wing and the legs are in split back stitch, using 934. I used 695 for the beak and the eye is outlined with **one strand** of 934.

Small bird on the right. I used 205 for the body, 695 for the beak and the wing is shaded in 693, 695 and 932. It is outlined with one strand of 932. The legs and outlining of the eye are made with **one strand** of 934.

The little flower on the right has leaves in 334 with veins in 332, petals in 203 and a centre of French knots, using **three strands** of 695.

COUNTED-THREAD INSECTS – OPTIONAL

Tudor samplers and other embroideries were often scattered with these charming motifs, sometimes used to cover flaws in the fabric or mistakes in the embroidery.

The insects charted on the page opposite are all worked in tent stitch, using **two strands** of perlé nr 5. You can use the photograph of the cushion on page 8 to place them among the embroidery, or

use only a few of them or none at all. The outlines and the details are worked in back stitch using **one strand** of dark brown perlé cotton, **after** the surrounding background has been worked.

COLOUR GUIDE – Appleton's crewel wool

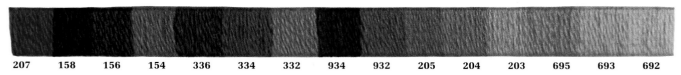

| 207 | 158 | 156 | 154 | 336 | 334 | 332 | 934 | 932 | 205 | 204 | 203 | 695 | 693 | 692 |

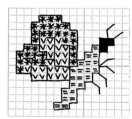

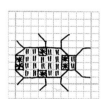

THE BARGELLO BORDER

It is most important to get the central area of the embroidery exactly the right size or the border will not fit together at the corners. The only way to do this is by counting the number of canvas threads along the outer edge of the central design. There should be 200 threads of canvas on the long dimension, and 172 threads along the short. (Check with sketch on page 10.)

Having established the exact inner measurements of the border, mark them with pins, then draw a

pencil line on the canvas in the groove outside the last thread in each direction. (You will have to miss out the places that have already been embroidered with leaves but make sure that the line runs straight through these areas.) Draw the two lines forming the outer edge of the border, carefully counting out 19 threads down as shown on the coloured chart on page 14.

If you want to work your own variations and still get the border to fit, the thread count for any one

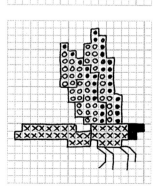

The yarn requirements on the right refer to the insect motifs, which can be used on the large cushion and the fire screen. The dragonfly motif is used on the scissor keeper on page 17.

YARN REQUIREMENTS
DMC perlé nr 5

Symbol	Colour	Amount
●	315	1 skein
○	407	1 skein
✳	918	1 skein
v	758	1 skein
×	924	1 skein
∕	502	1 skein
⊔	829	1 skein
▬	729	1 skein
⊻	580	1 skein
■	938	1 skein

COLOUR GUIDE – DMC perlé nr 5

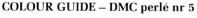

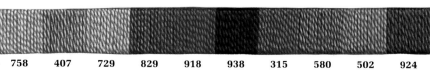

| 758 | 407 | 729 | 829 | 918 | 938 | 315 | 580 | 502 | 924 |

Work 1 line of long-legged cross stitch over 2 threads.

side has to be any multiple of 14 plus 18 – there are 14 canvas threads between each bargello peak and nine on each end.

Starting the bargello. Begin with the bottom part of the cushion, where the leaves don't encroach into the border. Find the centre point of the border by counting the threads and put a pencil mark in this groove. The green line worked in 336 forms the 'skeleton' of the bargello pattern. (Refer to chart opposite.) Use **four strands** of crewel wool and starting from the centre point of the border begin embroidering, working vertical straight stitches over two or four canvas threads. When you reach the corner there will be some stitches that work over 1 thread or over 3 threads to fit the diagonal line, as shown on the coloured chart. If you have counted and stitched correctly, you should arrive at the corner correctly. Do not begin embroidering the other colours before you are sure that your pattern runs correctly. Starting from the centre of the piece means that you will realise sooner if something has gone wrong. Once the bargello pattern is complete, fill in the small triangles near the edge with tent stitch, as shown in the chart (use **three strands** in the colour indicated).

All that remain are the two rows of long-legged cross stitch on the inner and outer edges of the border. Use **four strands** of crewel wool for these. You can now embark on the tent-stitch background.

Find the centre of the border and start at this point of the pattern.

Stretch and starch the embroidery (*see* page 113). Make up the cushion (*see* page 117). Hand over to a professional to be mounted as a fire screen.

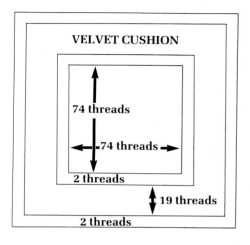

VELVET CUSHION

74 threads

74 threads

2 threads

19 threads

2 threads

THE BACKGROUND

Velvet cushion with embroidered panel. Overall size: 35 x 35 cm (14 x 14 in).

Start with the green and blue hills at the base of the central picture. **Three strands** of Appleton's crewel wool were used throughout and all the background was worked in diagonal tent stitch (*see* page 109). Each hill has three stripes with the lightest shade at the bottom. The green hills are worked in 336, 334 and 332. The blue hills are in 154, 156 and 158. Complete the rest of the background in diagonal tent stitch, using the gold nr 692. Tuck in the stitches close up to the embroidered motif so that the canvas doesn't show.

Once the background is complete finish off the outlines of the insects, as previously instructed.

VELVET CUSHION

- **You will need** *a 30 cm (12 in) square of size 14 interlock mono canvas*
- *Appleton's crewel wools in the shades and quantities given on page 11*
- *1 needle size 22*
- *embroidery frame*

The drawing on page 16 is exactly half-size. Enlarge it and copy it on to the canvas as previously instructed. The broken lines surrounding the motif are **guidelines** only.

The embroidery instructions are exactly the same as for the previous projects. The insects

were not used at all in this design. Refer to the sketch above to establish the exact thread count before starting the bargello border.

Stretch and starch (*see* page 113). The velvet cushion has mitred corners and was trimmed with purchased cord. See making-up instructions on pages 118–119.

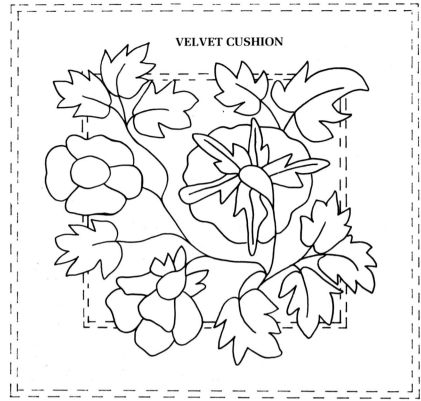

VELVET CUSHION

guideline only

THE SMALL PROJECTS

These small projects are designed to use up left-over yarn and canvas. The quantities required are minute. If you wish to make any of these objects by themselves, simply purchase one skein of each colour.

Wooden pincushion. Copy the drawing at top of page 17 on to the canvas as previously instructed. The base should be large enough to accommodate a 10 cm (4 in) circle of embroidery. The roses and background are worked exactly as in the large pieces. Refer to the partly worked example on page 10 to help you. Stretch and starch (see page 113) and mount according to manufacturer's instructions.

SCISSOR KEEPER

- **You will need** *a 10 x 20 cm (4 x 8 in) of size 18 interlock mono canvas*
- *small quantities of the relevant Appleton's crewel wools and DMC perlé cotton nr 5*
- *1 needle size 24*

The scissor keeper is charted on page 17. Also see instructions for the Victorian Pansy scissor keeper on page 26. The dragonfly uses **one strand** of perlé nr 5. (See yarn requirements on page 13.) Use **two strands** of Appleton's crewel wool for the diagonal tent stitch backgrounds (see page 109), and **three strands** of Appleton's for the long-legged cross stitch border (see page 110). The inner background is worked in

Appleton's crewel wool nr 692. The outer tent stitch area is in Appleton's 334. The long-legged cross stitch is in Appleton's 205. Complete the outlines of the dragonfly **after** the background.

Stretch and starch. Make up as per instructions on page 124. Use Appleton's 934 for the long-legged cross stitch seam. Make twisted cord ties (page 115) with left-over wool.

The pincushion on the right was made with scraps of left-over velvet. A small panel of bargello was inserted. See making-up instructions on page 120. The cushion was trimmed with twisted cord (page 115) and tied in knots at the corners. Overall size: 10 x 10 cm (4 x 4 in).

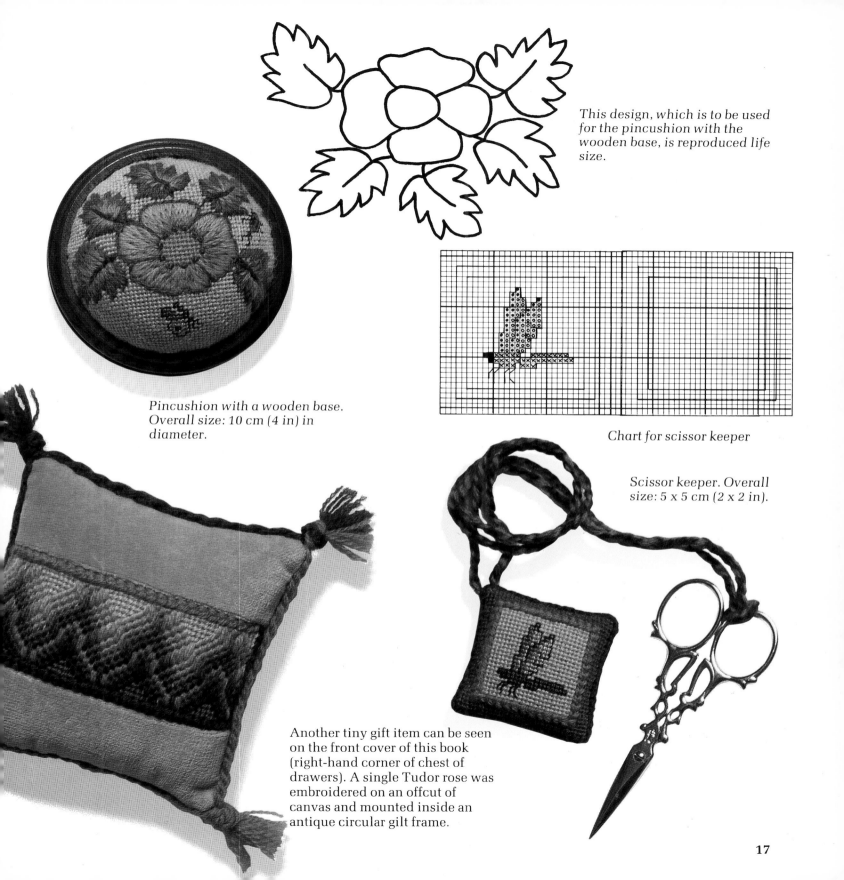

This design, which is to be used for the pincushion with the wooden base, is reproduced life size.

Pincushion with a wooden base. Overall size: 10 cm (4 in) in diameter.

Chart for scissor keeper

Scissor keeper. Overall size: 5 x 5 cm (2 x 2 in).

Another tiny gift item can be seen on the front cover of this book (right-hand corner of chest of drawers). A single Tudor rose was embroidered on an offcut of canvas and mounted inside an antique circular gilt frame.

VICTORIAN PANSIES

Canvas work – Berlin woolwork – enjoyed an unsurpassed popularity during the Victorian period. The craze attracted the attention of clever businessmen such as Sam Beeton, husband of the famed Mrs Beeton. He first imported from Germany, then produced the blank canvas; he pioneered the printing of pictures on canvas as well as selling charts and yarns. The term 'Berlin work' was used to describe a great variety of canvas work from the delicate to the very coarse. Houses were awash with it: furniture covers, rugs, cushions and an endless variety of knicknacks were covered with the ubiquitous Berlin work.

Some of the most popular and attractive patterns were floral

motifs. Pansies with their pretty faces and velvety petals were perfect subjects. They appeared on many artefacts such as fans and postcards – collecting postcards being another Victorian fashion – and on embroidered or woven textiles.

The glowing colours of freshly picked pansies were the inspiration for the objects in this section.

Figured taffeta cushion with a finely worked
inset. The round pincushion uses the centre motif
of the ivory cushion shown overleaf.

*Ivory coloured moire cushion
with large embroidered inset.
Overall size of cushion: 37 ×
37 cm (14½ × 14½ in).*

Figured taffeta with embroidered
inset. Overall size of cushion:
33 × 33 cm (13 × 13 in).

IVORY CUSHION – BURGUNDY CUSHION

- **You will need** **for the ivory cushion**
- *a 40 cm (16 in) square of size 12 interlock mono canvas*
- *Paterna Persian yarn in the shades and quantities given below*
- *1 needle size 20*
- *embroidery frame (optional)*

for the burgundy cushion
- *a 30 cm (12 in) square of size 18 interlock mono canvas*
- *DMC perlé nr 5 and Appleton's crewel wools in the shades and quantities given below*
- *1 needle size 22 or 24*
- *embroidery frame (optional)*

Use continental tent stitch for the motifs and diagonal tent stitch for the background. (See glossary of stitches on page 109.) Always work the motif before starting on the background.

The border. The chart only shows one complete corner. Turn the book through ninety degrees to start each corner design. I suggest you work the corner garland first, then fill in the trellis. I charted one garland **without** the trellis.

The ivory cushion. The chart for this design is shown opposite. Paterna Persian yarn has been used throughout on this piece. This is a three-stranded yarn. To achieve a smooth finish, take all three strands apart, then select the **two strands** you need to work the embroidery. In this way you will avoid working with two strands which are still twisted together. The final result will be smoother and more evenly tensioned.

Fold the canvas into four to find the centre and start working.

Pincushion on a wooden base

YARN REQUIREMENTS

	ivory cushion Paterna Persian yarn		burgundy cushion DMC perlé nr 5	
●	310	1 skein	550	1 skein
∧	311	1 skein	552	1 skein
⁄	312	1 skein	554	1 skein
▲	723	1 skein	977	1 skein
⊙	725	1 skein	725	1 skein
—	727	1 skein	726	1 skein
◥	870	1 skein	221	1 skein
×	871	1 skein	223	1 skein
∠	872	1 skein	224	1 skein
◣	650	1 skein	469	1 skein
⋈	652	1 skein	470	1 skein
⁄	653	1 skein	472	1 skein
■	420	1 skein	310	1 skein
·	261	1 skein	écru	1 skein
c	442	2 skeins	420	1 skein
⁄	443	2 skeins	422	1 skein
background	756	10 skeins	background Appleton's crewel wool 934	1 hank

22

The burgundy cushion has a double row of long-legged cross stitch.

This chart is for both cushions: use centre motif for the pincushion, using nr 470 for the background.

COLOUR GUIDE – Paterna Persian yarn – ivory cushion – pincushion

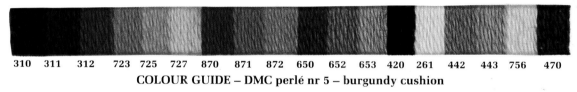

310 311 312 723 725 727 870 871 872 650 652 653 420 261 442 443 756 470

COLOUR GUIDE – DMC perlé nr 5 – burgundy cushion

550 552 554 977 725 726 221 223 224 469 470 472 420 422 310 écru Appleton's
crewel wool
934

23

1 row of long-legged cross stitch

COLOUR GUIDE – DMC stranded cotton

524   522   520   945   3064   632   677   676   783   3371   3743   3040   3041   3740   écru   white

DMC Médicis wool

For the outer border, work two rows of tent stitch. Complete with one row of long-legged cross stitch, using all **three strands** of the Paterna yarn.

Stretch and starch (*see* page 113). Turn to the making-up instructions on page 118.

The burgundy cushion. Work the flower and border patterns in continental tent stitch, using **one strand** of perlé cotton. The background is worked in diagonal tent stitch, using **two strands** of Appleton's crewel wool. The outer border is formed by two rows of long-legged cross stitch, using **three strands**. All other instructions are as for the ivory cushion.

YARN REQUIREMENTS
DMC stranded cotton

■	3371	1 skein
◣	520	1 skein
ᛪ	522	1 skein
⁄	524	1 skein
◥	632	1 skein
✕	3064	2 skeins
↵	945	1 skein
▲	783	1 skein
⊙	676	1 skein
−	677	1 skein
●	3740	1 skein
∧	3041	1 skein
⁄	3040	1 skein
·	3743	1 skein

background: DMC Médicis wool
écru or white: 7 skeins

WEDDING RING PILLOW

Wedding ring pillow. Overall size: 20 × 20 cm (8 × 8 in).

- **You will need**   a 35 cm (14 in) square of size 18 interlock mono canvas
- DMC stranded cotton and DMC Médicis wool in the shades and quantities given opposite
- 1 needle size 24
- embroidery frame (optional)

The cushion was made up using cream-coloured moire fabric, left over from the wedding gown. Therefore I chose écru to work the background of the embroidered panel. If the fabric is white, use white also for the background embroidery.

Initials and dates. The chart indicates their positioning on the cushion. You will need to work out the length of each word in order to centre them. *See Alphabet & Monograms section on page 106.*

Fold the canvas into four to find the centre. Begin work on the two centre hearts. All motifs, initials, names and numerals are worked in DMC stranded cotton, using all **six strands**. The background is made using **three strands** of DMC Médicis wool.

Complete all the embroidery before starting on the background. Finish off with one row of long-legged cross stitch, using **four strands** of Médicis wool. Stretch and starch as explained on page 113 and turn to make-up instructions on page 118.

NEEDLE BOOK & SCISSOR KEEPER

To make these two objects you will need two offcuts of size 18 interlock mono canvas, one measuring 25 x 15 cm (10 x 6 in) and the second 20 x 10 cm (8 x 4 in). use all **six strands** of DMC stranded cottons for the motifs and **three strands** of DMC Médicis wool for the backgrounds. Use one needle, size 24.

Scissor keeper. Fold the canvas in half to find the central thread. Work one row of long-legged cross stitch, as marked on the chart, to form the spine. Once this line is in place, it is easy to place the borders and the pansy motif. Tent stitch is used throughout. Stretch and starch as usual. Turn to making-up instructions on page 124.

Scissor keeper with twisted cord loop. Overall size: 5 x 5 cm (2 x 2 in).

Needle book with twisted cord ties. Overall size: 10 x 10 cm (4 x 4 in).

Chart for scissor keeper

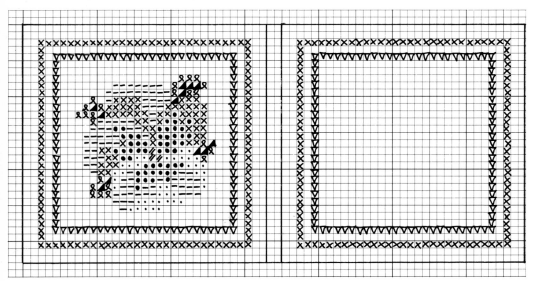

YARN REQUIREMENTS
DMC stranded cotton

●	3371	1 skein
◢	520	1 skein
ℵ	522	1 skein
✕	315	1 skein
—	316	1 skein
·	778	1 skein
⌀	783	1 skein
◔	676	1 skein
✎	677	1 skein
▽	3041	1 skein
╥	3042	1 skein
	background:	DMC Médicis wool
	8206	7 skeins

spine: 1 row of tent stitch

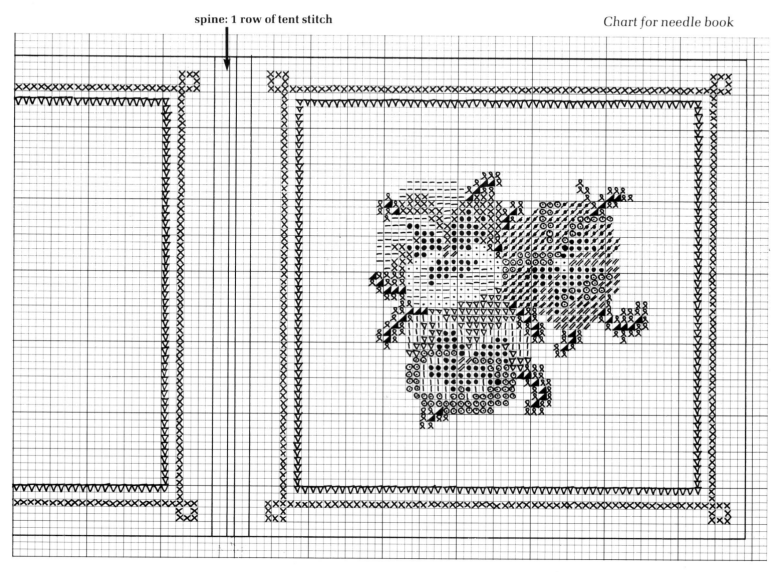

Needle book. Fold the canvas in half. Work a single row of tent stitch to form the spine. The needle book is eventually edged all round with long-legged cross stitch. This does not appear on the chart as it is done **after** the piece has been stretched and forms part of the making-up instructions on page 123.

The motifs and the borders are worked in continental tent stitch and the background in diagonal tent stitch. A monogram could be used on the back (see page 106).

COLOUR GUIDE – DMC stranded cotton

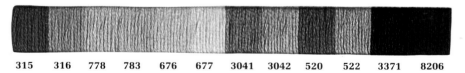

| 315 | 316 | 778 | 783 | 676 | 677 | 3041 | 3042 | 520 | 522 | 3371 | 8206 |

DMC Médicis wool

TUNISIAN IMAGES

The richly patterned tiles and the Islamic decorations on the copper plate were produced by Tunisian craftsmen. They feature a large, bold central motif, framed by smaller designs. These elegant patterns, which appear on a great variety of decorative artefacts, fill the souks with warm and rich colours. They were the starting point for the series of cushions, the footstool cover and other objects reproduced in this section.

Tile panel using the tree of life as the central motif. The blue and green glazes are typical of the Keruan area of Tunisia. The heavy brass plate is decorated with a central rosette, surrounded by stylised Arabic script.

A large footstool, a collection of cushions, and small accessories – all inspired by traditional Islamic patterns.

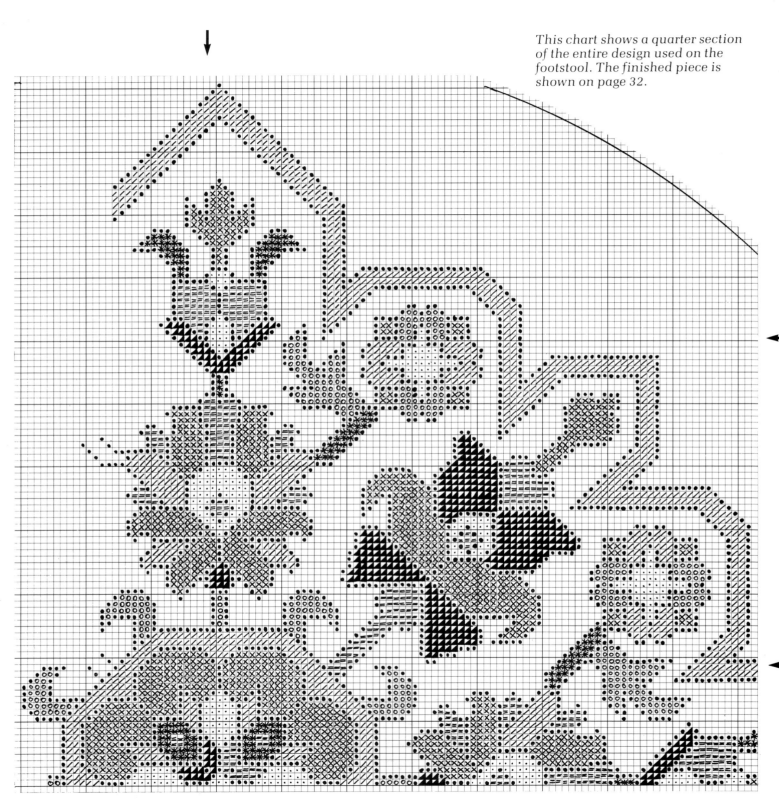

This chart shows a quarter section of the entire design used on the footstool. The finished piece is shown on page 32.

FOOTSTOOL WITH TUNISIAN MOTIF

- **You will need** *a 50 cm (20 in) square of size 14 interlock mono canvas*
- *Appleton's crewel wools and DMC perlé nr 3 (or 2 strands of perlé nr 5 if nr 3 is unavailable) in the shades and quantities given below*
- *1 needle size 22*
- *1 footstool base large enough to take a 41 cm (16 in) diameter piece of embroidery*
- *large compass/or a piece of string, a waterproof felt-tipped pen and a pin*
- *embroidery frame (optional)*

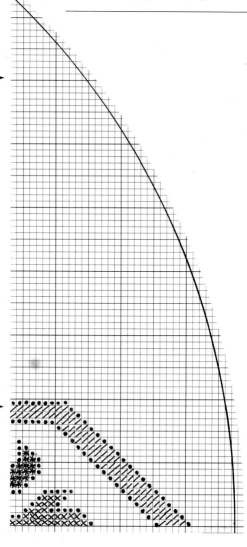

Find the centre of the piece of canvas by folding it into four. Open out and mark the centre. Draw a circle on the canvas with a radius of 20.5 cm (8 in) – 41 cm (16 in) across. If you do not have a large enough compass, use a piece of string and a pin. Lay the piece of canvas onto a board. Tie a knot at one end of the string, stick a pin through the knot and the centre point of the canvas and hold it steady. Measure 20·5 cm (8 in) along the string from the knot and make a mark at that point. Holding the knot with the pin with your left hand, place a pencil against the mark on the string and, using your right hand, draw a circle with the waterproof felt-tipped pen. Make sure to draw this circle before you start stitching as this will distort the canvas. This guideline will ensure that you stitch enough background to allow for the upholstering of the finished stool.

Three strands of Appleton's crewel wool are used throughout, except for the details in the motifs for which **1 strand** of nr 3 perlé cotton is used (or **2 strands** of nr 5).

YARN REQUIREMENTS
Appleton's crewel wool

Symbol	Colour	Quantity	DMC
●	934	1 hank	8124
◣	643	½ hank	8407
✕	866	½ hank	8126
✳	998	1 skein	8500
◪	695	2 hanks*	8303
◢	749	½ hank	8205
○	933	2 skeins	8136
⊡	DMC perlé nr 3 739	1 skein	
	inner background 693	1 hank	8313
	outer background 695	included in*	

COLOUR GUIDE – Appleton's crewel wool

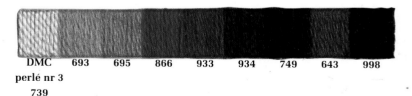

DMC perlé nr 3 739	693	695	866	933	934	749	643	998

This large footstool – its finished diameter is 45 cm (17¾ in) – is very popular with my ten-year-old daughter who loves sitting on it.

Start working from the centre of the piece, stitching the design outwards. First work the outline of the design in continental tent stitch. Then, using diagonal tent stitch, fill in the rest of the design and backgrounds.

The inner background is worked in the paler gold and the outer in the darker one.

When the embroidery is complete, stretch and starch it in the usual way (*see* page 113). I would recommend that you then take it and the stool base to an upholsterer to have the piece professionally mounted.

The design would also look magnificent on a chair seat or a piano stool. It is easy to adapt the chart for a square or oblong seat as the central motif does not change. It is only the shape and size of the outer background which will require altering.

To position the motif, it is best to make a paper template of the seat you wish to cover. Draw the outline of the shape on to the canvas, remembering to allow an extra margin for turn-overs. Find the centre of the canvas and begin work on the motif in the usual way.

You will need to increase the quantity of canvas and dark gold yarn (Appleton's 695) accordingly.

CUSHION – DESIGN I – TWO COLOURWAYS

These two cushions feature the same design and are worked from the chart on page 35. They are worked in two colourways to suit a variety of interiors and individual taste. Each cushion is designed to marry up with another different yet compatible motif, as shown on page 36. This second design too has been worked in both colourways.

The brighter colour scheme uses hues similar to those of traditional hand-woven rugs and will look wonderful with bold, warm colours, while the more subdued version will team up better with a more conventional, feminine setting.

See *chart and yarn requirements overleaf. Overall size of each cushion: 38 x 38cm (15 x 15 in).*

33

- **You will need** *a 40 cm (16 in) square of size 14 interlock mono canvas*
- *Appleton's crewel wools and DMC perlé nr 3, or 2 strands of perlé nr 5 if nr 3 is unavailable, in the shades and quantities given below*
- *1 needle size 22*
- *embroidery frame (optional)*

The chart for the cushion design is shown opposite and has been partly coloured to make it easier to follow. The coloured sections of the chart should be worked in Appleton's crewel wool nr 866 in the case of the red cushion, and in nr 206 for the pink one.

Find the centre of the canvas by folding into four. Start working from the centre of the design. First work the outlines of the motif in continental tent stitch, using **three strands** of Appleton's crewel wool. Fill in the backgrounds in diagonal tent stitch, also using **three strands** of the wool. The small details are worked in **one strand** of DMC perlé. The whole piece is outlined with one row of long-legged cross stitch, using **four strands** of Appleton's crewel wool.

When the embroidery is complete, stretch and starch the piece (see page 113). Make up the cushion according to the instructions on page 118.

YARN REQUIREMENTS – Appleton's crewel wool

	pink colourway	red colourway		DMC
	206	866	1½ hanks	8126
	154	749	½ hank	8205
	931	933	2 skeins	8136
	693	693	1 skein	8313
	343	643	2 skeins	8407
	974	934	1 hank	8124
	DMC perlé nr 3 739	DMC perlé nr 3 739	1 skein	

The coloured areas on the chart are stitched in **206** for the pink cushion and in **866** for the red cushion.

The uncoloured inner background is stitched in **984** for the pink cushion and **692** for the red cushion (½ hank in either case).

COLOUR GUIDE – Appleton's crewel wool – pink colourway

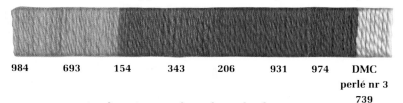

984   693   154   343   206   931   974   DMC perlé nr 3 739

Appleton's crewel wool – red colourway

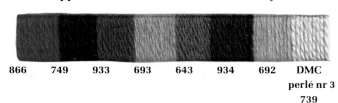

866   749   933   693   643   934   692   DMC perlé nr 3 739

First design — either colourway

The area contained between arrows is a quarter section of the design.

CUSHION – SECOND DESIGN – TWO COLOURWAYS

This cushion is to be made up in exactly the same way as the previous pair (*see* instructions on page 118).

Please note that the yarn requirements for the previous cushion, given on page 34, also apply to this design.

This is the companion design which will form a pair with the cushion illustrated on page 33. As before, it appears worked in two colourways. The relevant chart is shown opposite. As instructed before, the coloured sections of the chart should be worked in Appleton's crewel wool nr 866 in the case of the red cushion, and in nr 206 for the pink one.

36

Chart – second design

The area contained within arrows is a quarter section of the design.

DESIGNS I AND II – SUGGESTIONS FOR FURTHER USES

Because of their geometric shapes, the two designs used in the pair of cushions shown in earlier pages are easily repeatable. Choose one of the two motifs, repeat it to make an attractive cover for a duet piano stool or repeat it three times to cover a fender stool. Using the red colourway or choosing a colour scheme to your own taste, a magnificent rug could be made by repeating and alternating both designs and combining them with the border used around the chess board, charted on page 70. A detail of this border is shown below. The repeats in the pattern within the border are easily worked out, using graph paper, and the existing chart shows how to turn the corner.

The footstool design on page 32 could be used for a pair of carver chairs, and the cushion designs alternated to create a stunning set of dining chair seats.

Detail of the border on the chessboard on page 69. This detail is shown life-size.

DOORSTOP

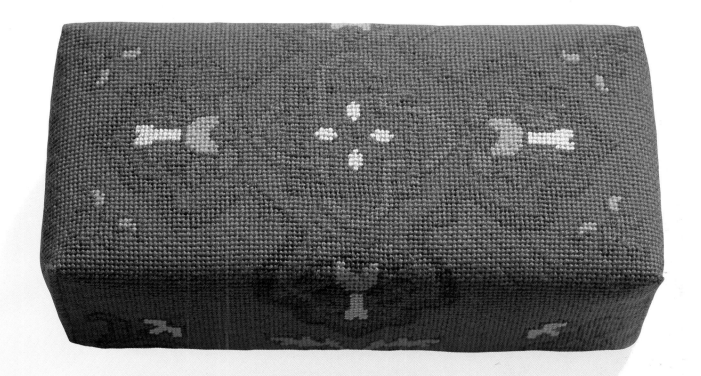

Doorstop made by covering a standard house brick with a piece of embroidery compatible in design with either cushion.

- **You will need**   a 50 x 40 cm (20 x 16 in) oblong of size 14 interlock mono canvas
- Appleton's crewel wools and DMC perlé nr 3 in the shades and quantities given overleaf.
- 1 size 22 needle
- embroidery frame (optional)
- 1 standard house brick 21·5 x 7·5 x 10 cm (8½ x 3 x 4 in)

Fold the canvas into four to find the centre. Begin from the central point of the motif, working the outline first, using continental tent stitch.

Fill in the inner part of the motifs and the background with diagonal tent stitch.

Use **three strands** of Appleton's wools and **one strand** of perlé.

Repeat the back panel and the small side panel. When the embroidery is complete, stretch and starch the piece and turn to page 122 to find out how to finish off the doorstop.

YARN REQUIREMENTS – Appleton's crewel wool

	pink colourway	red colourway	
⊠	154	749	½ hank
·	931	933	2 skeins
⊿	693	693	1 skein
∧	343	643	2 skeins
●	974	934	½ hank
	background 206	background 866	2 hanks
☰	DMC perlé nr 3 739	DMC perlé nr 3 739	1 skein

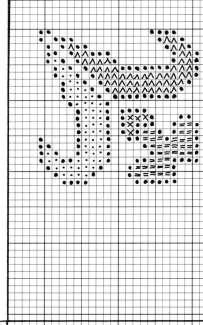

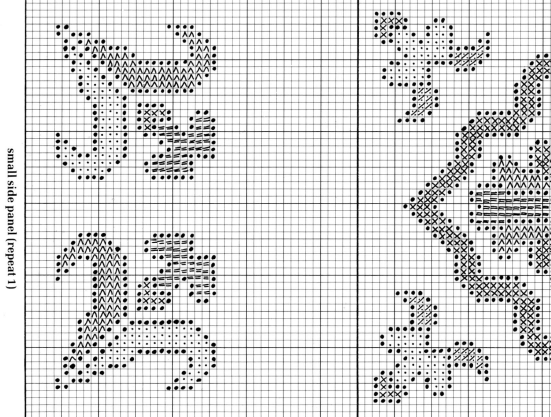

small side panel (repeat 1)

Chart for doorstop

large side panel (repeat 1)

centre

top of the doorstop (1 only)

NEEDLEBOOK & SCISSOR KEEPER

The needlebook illustrated below and charted opposite is different on the front and the back. Alone, or with a scissor/key keeper, it makes an attractive and easy-to-make gift.

The cushions on pages 33 and 36 were worked in two colourways; the same can be done with these smaller items. They are also an excellent way of using up odds and ends of canvas and wool. Please note that the yarn requirements listed below will yield one needlebook **and** one scissor or key keeper in either colourway. For the needlebook you will need one offcut of size 14 white interlock canvas, measuring 15 x 30 cm (6 x 12 in). The keepers will each require an oblong 20 x 10 cm (8 x 4 in) of the same size of canvas.

Finished size of needlebook: 10 x 10 cm (4 x 4 in).

The front and the back of the needlebook are reproduced below. You could of course choose the motif you like best and keep the back plain, or work a monogram in the centre (*see* alphabet section on page 106).

Use **three strands** of Appleton's crewel wool and **one strand** of perlé wherever specified.

The scissor or key keeper is charted opposite. These tiny 'cushions' are attractive hanging from a clock's or cabinet's key, they can be used as lavender sachets, as cushions in a doll's house, or as Christmas tree gifts.

YARN REQUIREMENTS – Appleton's crewel wool

	pink colourway	red colourway	
/	206	866	1 hank
×	154	749	1 skein
·	931	933	1 skein
∕	693	693	1 skein
∧	343	643	1 skein
●	974	934	2 skeins
	*inner background (keepers) 984	*inner background (keepers) 692	1 skein
=	DMC perlé nr 3 739	DMC perlé nr 3 739	1 skein

*All other backgrounds are worked in **206** for the pink colourway and in **866** for the red.

The front and back of the needlebook have different motifs.

The scissor keeper has been worked in the pink colourway to match the needlebook.

Chart for the needlebook.

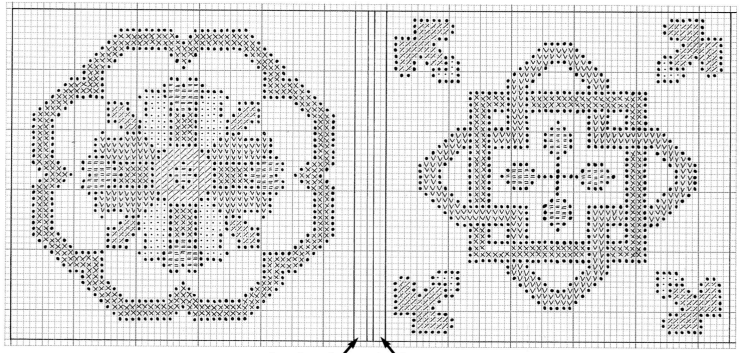

long-legged cross stitch in 866 or 206

The key keeper was worked in the red version.

Chart for the scissor or key keeper.

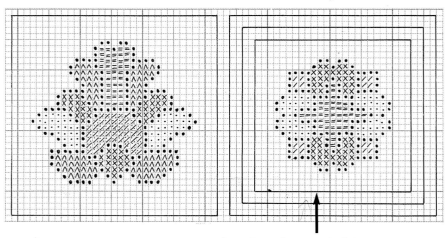

long-legged cross stitch in 749 or 154

SHAKESPEARIAN FLOWERS

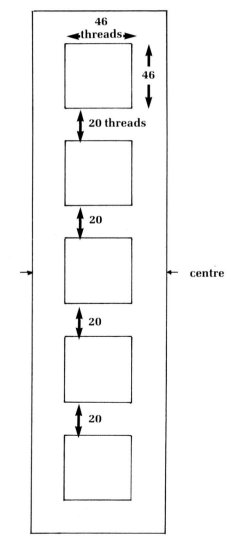

Cushion with antique embroidered flowers, mounted on velvet.

During the seventeenth century it became fashionable to embroider random motifs – flowers or animals – on to linen. These would then be cut and applied to furnishings or garments. There is a spectacular set of bed hangings which can be seen at Hampton Court Palace. The bright colours of the floral motifs have remained amazingly vivid. Floral motifs were particularly popular at the time and reflect the contemporary passion for garden design. The flowers are often worked in a highly realistic fashion and provide a good record of the garden plants which were popular at the time.

For this reason, I have called this section Shakespearian Flowers. The antique cushion shown above has a lily as a central motif which is worked in long-and-short stitch. I have reinterpreted the design, but it was the starting point for the series of objects contained in this chapter.

44

Bell pull embroidered in long-and-short stitch. Overall size: 62 x 13 cm (25 x 5 in).

The sketch opposite shows the arrangement of the flowers embroidered in long-and-short stitch as used in the bell pull.

THE BELL PULL

- **You will need** *a 80 x 25 cm (32 x 10 in) oblong of size 14 interlock mono canvas*
- *Appleton's crewel wools and DMC perlé nr 5 in the shades and quantities given on page 46*
- *1 needle size 22*
- *embroidery frame*
- *1 set of brass bell-pull ends**

* Antique ones were used for the example illustrated on the previous page but attractive modern alternatives are easily found

Fold the canvas in half to find the centre, as shown on the diagram on page 44.

Counting the threads, draw in pencil on the canvas the five squares shown in the diagram. Ensure that you have counted the threads accurately or the border will not fit.

The next step is to draw the flowers. The drawings are shown life-size on the next five pages. Trace these on to paper first. You will then be able to lay them out flat and superimpose the canvas with the pencil-drawn boxes over the individual drawings. Line up the pencil line on the canvas with the broken line on the drawing. Using a waterproof felt-tipped pen, trace the first flower drawing on to the canvas. (The pen MUST be waterproof: check it on a spare piece of canvas, as you could ruin the piece of work when it is dampened for stretching.) A medium thickness pen is best. Do not press too hard in order to draw smooth lines.

Repeat for all four flowers, down the length of the bell pull.

The embroidery is worked in the following order: flowers and leaves, then their stamens and veining; the line of dark tent stitch which frames the flowers; the green and mauve border. (See chart and instructions on page 52.) Fill in the pale gold background. The flower names are worked in back stitch, over the embroidered background. Finally, the piece is enclosed with one row of long-legged cross stitch.

Use **three strands** of Appleton's wool throughout, except for the border pattern which uses **four strands**, and the outlining on all the flower petals, which takes **one strand**. Where perlé is stipulated, use **one strand**.

YARN REQUIREMENTS – Appleton's crewel wool*

221	1 skein	332	1 skein
222	1 skein	334	½ hank
223	1 skein	336	½ hank
224	1 skein	882	1 skein
932	½ hank	692	2 hanks
934	2 skeins	693	1 skein
695	1 skein	DMC perlé nr 5 3371	1 skein

*To work the flowers individually as pictures (pages 50 and 53), you will need 1 skein of each colour specified for your chosen flower and ½ hank of 692 for the background; 1 skein each of 932, 934, and 334 for the border.

COLOUR GUIDE – Appleton's crewel wool

882   692   693   695   332   334   336   932   934   221   222   223   224   DMC perlé nr 5 3371

The rose. The petals are worked in long-and-short stitch, using three shades of pink. The photographic detail below should help you. Start at the outer edges of the petals using nr 221 and make your first row of stitches. They should be slightly longer than seems necessary as will be shortened when you work the next shade into this first layer of stitches. Make sure that you work a stitch into every canvas hole, around the edge of all the petals. In order to do this and lay the threads in the right direction, you will need to overlap the stitches around the centre of the flower. Work two further rows of shading in 222 and 223. As you work each successive layer of shading, always split a thread of the stitch already on the canvas to ensure successful blending of the shades.

The two turned-up petal edges are worked in 223. The centre of the flower is first filled with diagonal tent stitch and then covered with French knots.

The leaves are worked in long-and-short stitch using nr 334. Here, too, make sure you use every canvas hole around the edge and overlap the stitches in the centre. The veins are worked in split back stitch in 332. The stem is split back stitch in 336, working several rows to fill the lines. The thorns are worked in perlé. Finally, outline the petals with split back stitch, using nr 224.

This drawing is reproduced life-size.

Detail of rose motif, showing the layers of stitches.

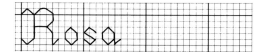

*Chart for the flower name. Remember that it has to be worked **over** the embroidered background.*

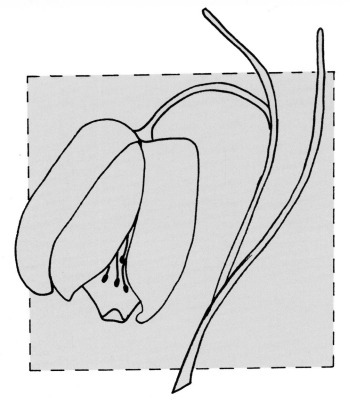

This drawing is shown life-size.

Detail of the motif.

The fritillary. Work all the petals in long-and-short stitch, using nr 932, and the inside of the flower in 934. Next outline the petals in split back stitch, using 934. The dark markings on the petals are made of groups of three straight stitches, worked in **one strand** of 934, over the long-and-short stitch area which forms the petals. Work the stamens in split back stitch and French knots, using **one strand** of 695.

The stalk and leaves are in long-and-short stitch worked in 334, using the lighter shade – 332 – towards the ends of the leaves.

Chart for the flower name. Work **after** completing the background.

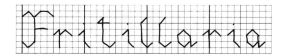

The lily. The longer petals to the right and left are worked in long-and-short stitch, using 882. The remaining four petals are shaded in 882, 693 and 695. The stamens are worked using **one strand** of perlé in split back stitch with a group of three French knots at the end of each.

The leaves are worked in satin stitch, using 334. The veins and stem are in split back stitch using 332. The petals are outlined in **one strand** of 692.

Drawing (life-size).

*Name chart (worked **over** background).*

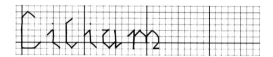

Detail of the lily.

Drawing (life-size)

The columbine motif was also worked singly and framed as a picture. The border is charted on page 52.

The columbine. The lower petals are shaded in 221, 222 and 223 and their edges are outlined in 221. The darker upper-pointed ends are in 223. The mauve top petals are in 932 and the veins in 934. They are outlined in split back stitch worked in 934.

The leaf is shaded in long-and-short stitch, using 332 and 334. The stem and veins are worked in split back stitch, using 336.

If you wish to make this flower into an individual picture, as shown below, complete the border and the background as instructed on page 52. Stretch and starch in the usual way, then take the picture to your framer to have it professionally mounted.

The pansy. See drawing on page 51. The top two petals are shaded, using 934, 932, 695 and 693. The remaining three petals have turned-over edges in 934 and are then shaded in 695, 693 and with **one strand** of perlé towards the centre of the flower. All the petals are then outlined in split back stitch in 934. The small dark areas between the petals are in perlé.

There are five French knots in the centre of the pansy.

*Name chart (worked **over** background)*

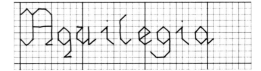

The leaves are shaded in 334 and 332. The veins and stems are split back stitch, worked in 336.

The pansy too was made up into an individual picture, as can be seen on page 53. It was finished and mounted as explained for the columbine.

Embroidered flower names. After filling the background to the flowers on the bell pull, you will want to work the Latin names of the flowers. There are 18 rows of tent stitch between each flower square. The base line of each word should be placed on row nine (i.e. in the middle of the gap). The words begin four stitches from the edge of the mauve and green border. The letters are worked in **one strand** of 336.

Drawing (life-size)

Follow the individual charts for working the names, using back stitch worked over a single canvas thread. Do not be tempted to make the stitches bigger, even in the straight descendants of the letters, as it would look coarse.

Finally, work a row of long-legged cross stitch outside the pale gold background area, using **three strands** of Appleton's crewel wool in 336.

*Name chart (worked **over** background)*

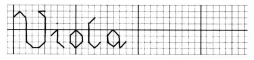

The borders. The pencil line that you made, enclosing 46 canvas threads, forms a box which contains each flower. Work a single row of continental tent stitch on the thread immediately outside this pencil line, using 934. Elements of the flowers or leaves will break through this line.

The chart below shows the border enclosing a single flower (see framed picture of pansy opposite). To adapt this border to fit around the bell-pull design, start at the top, following the chart which shows you how to work the corner. The photographic detail shown next to the chart should help you to see how the border is worked. Counting from the top left-hand corner, you will need to repeat the mauve and green motif 33 times to contain the design.

The background. Draw a pencil line two canvas threads away from the outer edge of the green and mauve border pattern. This marks the extent of the background. Fill in the whole area in pale gold 692, using diagonal tent stitch. As you work close up to the flowers and leaves, tuck your stitches in under the long-and-short stitch or the split back-stitch outlines, so that the canvas does not show through.

Complete the design with a single row of long-legged cross stitch. Finally, stretch and starch (see page 113) in the usual way or follow the manufacturer's instructions on how to mount the bell-pull ends.

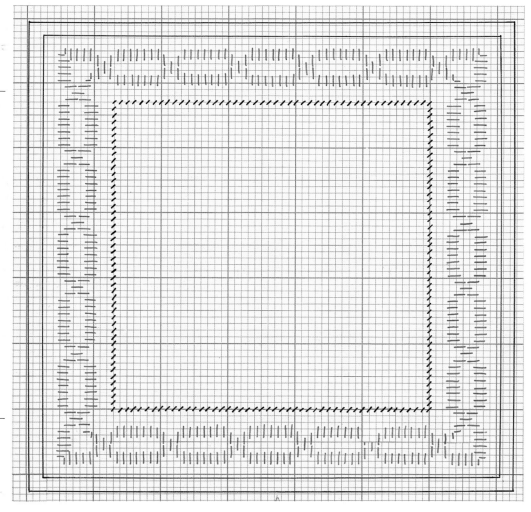

33 repeats for bell pull

This chart shows the border used around the pictures. It can easily be adapted for the bell pull.

CHART SYMBOLS –
Appleton's crewel wool

932

334

934

Detail of border

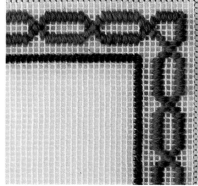

COLOURS FROM THE ORIENT

The fragment of an old rug shown above was the inspiration behind the decorative braid designs used for the objects featured in this section. I found the old golds and pinks present in the rug most appealing and included them in my own colour scheme.

I have always been fascinated by the way in which several borders of different width are combined in oriental rugs to form a major border pattern. By careful juxtaposition of designs and colours, widely differing effects can be achieved. The glowing, yet soft, palette of colours found in old rugs is not always easy to recreate, using modern embroidery wools. The chosen colour scheme for the projects used here was arrived at after a great deal of trial and error. Putting skeins of wool next to each other is not always sufficient and I frequently make subtle shade changes after working a sample of the design. I don't start the real thing until I am completely happy.

Cushion with embroidered inset, tasselled bolster
with embroidered braid and evening bag.

ORIENTAL CUSHION

- **You will need** *a 30 x 50 cm (12 x 20 in) oblong of size 14 interlock mono canvas*
- *Appleton's crewel wool was used throughout in the shades and quantities stated in the yarn requirement given below*
- *1 needle size 22*
- *embroidery frame (optional)*

The cushion reproduced opposite has a large panel made up of various border designs. The chart shown overleaf will enable you to make this cushion, as well as the evening bag illustrated on page 60. These pieces are worked entirely in tent stitch. As usual, start with the outlines of the motifs and work them in continental tent stitch, then fill in the shapes and the background, using diagonal tent stitch.

The entire piece is worked using **three strands** of Appleton's crewel wool.

The chart. I have hand-coloured some portions of the chart to make it easier to follow. As some of the shades appear both within a motif and as a background colour in another part of the design, the said colour – say mauve – is represented on the chart by the colour mauve in some sections and by a bold dot (.) where the mauve forms part of a motif.

As a rule, you will probably find it easier, when working border designs such as these, to start the embroidery from the top edge of the main panel and work down, rather than from the centre of the embroidery as is usual.

The whole design is outlined with a row of long-legged cross stitch, as shown on the chart.

As the embroidered panel forms, relatively speaking, a small part of the actual cushion, it is particularly important to spend time finding fabric that will complement the colour scheme. I was lucky to find a linen crash which teamed up extremely well, in colour as well as in texture, with the rich hues of the embroidery. Similarly, the blue piping matched the blue in the embroidery.

There is almost as much joy in searching for and finding just the right kind of fabric to complete a

piece, as in creating and working the embroidery. I never feel guilty about buying remnants of fabric for which I do not have an immediate use, as they always, sooner or later, prove to be just the finishing touch to a piece of work.

After completing the embroidery, stretch and starch the piece as usual and follow the make-up instructions on page 120.

YARN REQUIREMENTS
Appleton's crewel wool

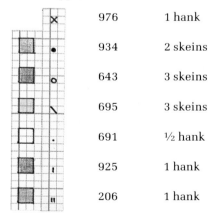

×	976	1 hank
●	934	2 skeins
○	643	3 skeins
\	695	3 skeins
.	691	½ hank
ı	925	1 hank
ıı	206	1 hank

COLOUR GUIDE – Appleton's crewel wool

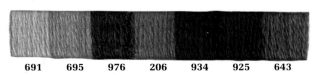

| 691 | 695 | 976 | 206 | 934 | 925 | 643 |

Cushion with embroidered inset. Overall size 40 x 40 cm (15¾ x 15¾ in).

start here

The chart reproduced on this spread enables you to complete
the cushion inset and the evening bag.

long-legged cross stitch in 925

EVENING BAG

- **You will need** *(in addition to the requirements listed for the cushion on page 56)*
- *a piece of matching fabric (moire, satin or silk) to line the bag, measuring 45 x 25 cm (18 x 10 in) – includes seam allowance*
- *1 button*
- *1 m (1 yd) of matching cord (optional)*

This bag is made from the same chart (see previous page) as the embroidery panel inset in the cushion illustrated on page 57. The bag is formed by folding the panel of embroidery into three.

Since this piece will not be mounted on another object, like the panel in the cushion for instance, it is important that it is well stretched and starched (see page 113). This is to ensure that the embroidery is absolutely square or the bag will tend to twist and distort. If in doubt, let a professional take charge of the stretching and starching.

When the embroidery is fully dry, following the starching process, trim the excess canvas, leaving a 2 cm (¾ in) margin all round the embroidery. The long-legged cross stitch tends to form a 'natural' edge and you will find it easy to fold over the excess canvas. With a herringbone stitch, attach the edge of unstitched canvas to the back of the work area. Do not pull the thread too tight: you should only catch through the wool at the back of the work, or the stitches will show on the right side of the embroidery.

Embroidered evening bag. Size of closed bag: 14 x 19 cm (5½ x 7½ in).

To form the bag, fold the bottom third of the embroidery over. Using two strands of the blue wool, carefully catch the two rows of long-legged cross stitch together. Make sure the ends of the seam are secure.

The lining. Lay the rectangle of lining, right side up, lengthwise in front of you. Fold one third of the cloth over to form a pocket (as shown in the sketch below), and stitch the two side seams.

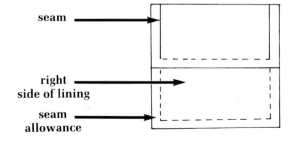

seam

right side of lining

seam allowance

Press seams open. Tuck the pocket inside the bag. The wrong side of the embroidery should butt against the wrong side of the lining. Turn in the seam allowance of the lining, pin or tack it to the front of the bag and around the flap, making sure it lies flat and does not pull. Slip-stitch the lining with matching thread, using a fine needle.

Attach a button to the front of the bag and, using two or three strands of the blue wool, make a buttonhole loop, matching the size of the selected button.

The bag can be used as a clutch bag, but if you prefer, you can make a twisted cord, as in the version illustrated here, or purchase a length of cord or a metallic chain.

Right. *Tasselled bolster. Length: 50 cm (20 in), diameter: 18 cm (7 in).*

ORIENTAL TASSELLED BOLSTER

The design already used for the cushion, and for the evening bag opposite, is composed of a series of borders placed side by side to form a panel. Here the various border patterns have been used to form braids which I mounted individually.

The middle braid on the bolster is made up of the three smaller border patterns, as can be seen in the detail shown below left. The chart used for the cushion and the evening bag and reproduced on the previous spread gives you all the information you need to complete the three braids.

As before, use **three strands** of Appleton's crewel wool.

To finish off the edges of the braids, I have added one row of long-legged cross stitch framed by one row of tent stitch

on either side. (See the photographic detail opposite.) The colour for these finishing touches should be decided in relation to the cloth you intend using to make up the bolster. After completing the three braids, stretch and starch as usual.

On page 120, you will find general instructions on how to make up a bolster. Quite deliberately, I have omitted to give exact measurements as most people will want to make a bolster to fit a particular piece of furniture. Similarly, I cannot give exact yarn quantities, as these will depend on the length of braid you wish to make and whether you wish to repeat them. The pieces of braid I have made for the bolster illustrated above only cover about ⅔ of the total circumference. The yarn requirements specified on page 56 will yield three 38 cm (15 in) long braids.

Instructions for making the tassels are located on page 115. The tassels look impressive, yet are easy to make and provide a nice 'professional' finish to the piece.

MAGIC CARPET

The extraordinary rug shown below is a fine example of the work of the nomadic Kurdish tribesmen living in the Armenian-Kazak region. This type of rug is often known as 'eagle Kazak'. This specimen dates from the mid-nineteenth century. I adapted the large cruciform centre motif for the cushion shown opposite. The red and white flowers were worked into the border of the cushion and of the chessboard. The same floral motif also gave the design used for the dressing table accessories on page 73.

Right. A cushion, chessboard and a variety of artefacts using traditional rug patterns.

THE GEOMETRIC CUSHION

- **You will need** *a 50 cm (20 in) square of size 14 interlock mono canvas*
- *Appleton's crewel wools in the shades and quantities given below*
- *1 needle size 22*
- *embroidery frame (optional)*

The cushion reproduced opposite has a large embroidered inset panel which would be big enough to mount as a cushion in its own right, without the blue cloth surround which was used for this version. The traditional Kazak rug design would look good in a variety of decors. On the previous page, you can see the cushion in a fairly modern setting but it would fit equally well with more traditional furnishings.

The clean geometric design makes this range of objects particularly suitable as gifts to a man; furthermore an increasing number of men appear to have discovered the therapeutic effects of needlepoint. I also had this in mind when I designed this cushion and the range of objects derived from it.

The chart on page 66 shows the centre motif of the cushion and a portion of the border is charted opposite it. Fold the canvas in four to find the centre, as marked on the chart. Start the embroidery from the centre of the motif, working the outlines first. These are worked in continental tent stitch (*see* page 109). The motifs and the backgrounds are then completed in diagonal tent stitch (*see* page 109). Use **three strands** of Appleton's crewel wools throughout.

When the embroidery is completed, stretch and starch the piece as instructed on page 113. The cushion can then be made up, following instructions on page 118.

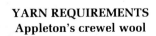

YARN REQUIREMENTS
Appleton's crewel wool

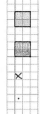

721	2 skeins
696	½ hank
926	½ hank
725	2 hanks
692	1 hank
643	2 skeins
998	2 hanks

COLOUR GUIDE – Appleton's crewel wool

| 692 | 696 | 725 | 721 | 643 | 926 | 998 |

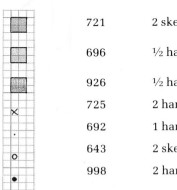

Right. Geometric cushion with traditional Kazak patterns. Overall size: 45 x 45 cm (18 x 18 in).

centre

The red lines are repeated on the chart and on the central motif chart. This is to help you to place the border correctly.

The chart on the right represents one half of a side of the border, and its corner. To position this section of the border in relation to the central motif, charted on the page opposite, match the centre point markings. Repeat the design for each corner of the cushion.

THE CHESSBOARD

- **You will need** *a 60 cm (24 in) square of size 14 interlock mono canvas*
- *Appleton's crewel wools in the shades and quantities given below*
- *1 needle size 22*
- *embroidery frame (optional)*

The chart for the chessboard appears overleaf. It shows a corner of the border design and the beginning of the checker design. The small diagram inset into the chart shows how the light and dark squares alternate.

The whole piece is worked in tent stitch, apart from the one row of long-legged cross stitch between the border and the checker board, as shown on the chart. Use **three strands** of Appleton's crewel wool throughout.

Measure 5 cm (2 in) from the edge of the canvas and start embroidering from the corner of the chart, working the outlines of the geometric motifs in continental tent stitch. The motifs and their background can then be filled in, using diagonal tent stitch (see page 109).

Work the amount of border shown on the chart and start work on the checker board, using the black and white diagram as a guideline. Note that the gold grid line around the squares should be worked in continental tent stitch. The black and white squares themselves can be filled in with diagonal tent stitch. Make sure you have the required number of squares, then complete the patterned border.

When the embroidery is complete, stretch and starch the piece and hand it over to a professional framer to mount according to your taste.

On the left is a picture of a matching box to contain the chessmen. You will find a chart for this design on page 72.

Right. Chessboard framed by a border taken from the cushion design on page 65. Overall size: 50 x 50 cm (20 x 20 in).

Box to contain chessmen. Overall size: 10 x 23 cm (4 x 9 in).

YARN REQUIREMENTS
Appleton's crewel wool

▧	721	1 skein
▨	696	1 hank*
▨	926	½ hank
×	725	2 hanks
.	692	3 hanks
o	643	1 skein
●	998	3 hanks
✳	696	included in*

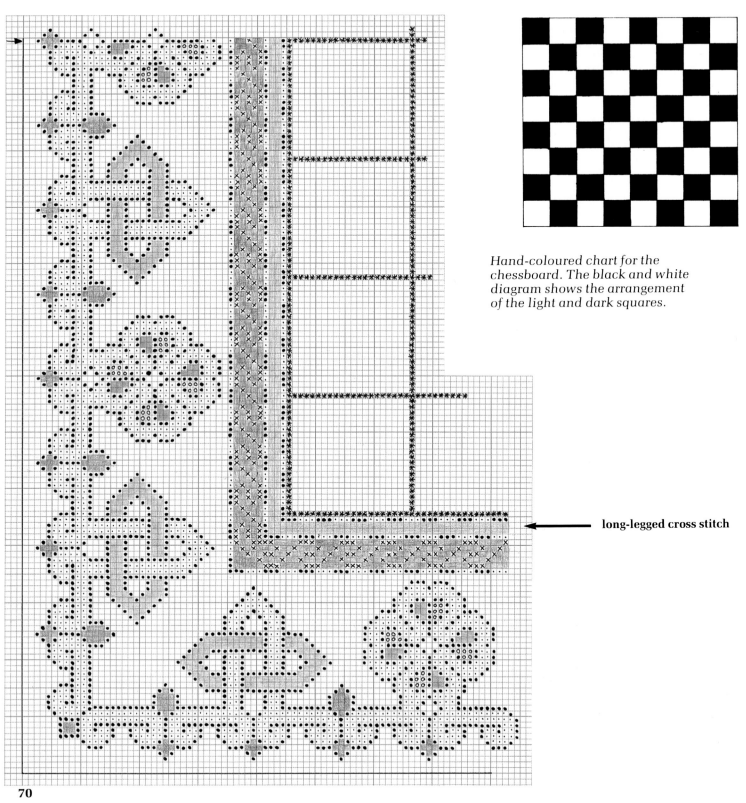

Hand-coloured chart for the
chessboard. The black and white
diagram shows the arrangement
of the light and dark squares.

long-legged cross stitch

70

THE CHESSMEN'S BOX & OTHER GIFT ITEMS

- **You will need for the chessmen's box:**
- *a 20 x 30 cm (8 x 12 in) oblong of size 14 interlock mono canvas*
- *Appleton's crewel wools in the shades and quantities given overleaf*
- *1 needle size 22*
- *1 ready-made wooden box large enough to accommodate the chess pieces*

- **For the credit card holder:**
- *same as above, omitting box*
- *a 20 x 30 cm (8 x 12 in) piece of lining material*

- **For the spectacle case:**
- *2 20 x 30 cm (8 x 12 in) oblongs of size 14 interlock mono canvas*
- *Appleton's crewel wools in the shades and quantities given overleaf*
- *1 needle size 22*

motif is dependent on the size of box obtainable from your local supplier. The motif can also be repeated side by side to produce a square box, for instance.

The same chart will also enable you to produce the credit card holder and the spectacle case illustrated below.

On page 68 there is a picture of a box matching the chessboard and designed to contain the chessmen. Of course, this box could be used for a variety of other purposes. The chart overleaf shows you part of the motif. The amount of red background you work around the

Spectacle case. Overall size:
19 x 8.5 cm (7.5 x 3.5 in).

Credit card holder. Overall size:
10 x 7.5 cm (4 x 3 in).

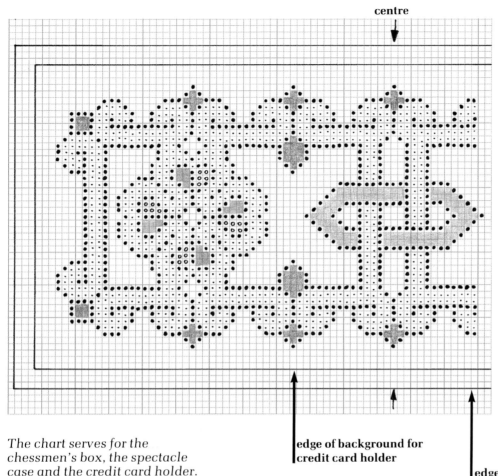

centre

The chart serves for the chessmen's box, the spectacle case and the credit card holder.

edge of background for credit card holder

edge of background for spectacle case

The lid of the chessmen's box, the credit card holder and the spectacle case are all stitched in exactly the same way.

Fold the canvas in four to find the centre. Start working the design in outline from the centre, using continental tent stitch.

Fill in the inner part of the motif and the red background in diagonal tent stitch. **Three strands** of Appleton's crewel wool have been used throughout.

To complete the box, simply follow the instructions supplied by the manufacturer.

The credit card holder is made up in exactly the same way as the evening bag on page 60, but omitting the button.

Assemble spectacle case following instructions given on page 123.

The stylized floral motif in the antique Kazak rug shown on page 62 inspired the pattern used for the series of objects pictured over the next few pages. The embroidery was combined with a rich warm russet-coloured raw silk to complement the oak dressing table top.

Whereas the last section featured objects which would make ideal masculine gifts, this series of artefacts is more feminine and yet uncluttered. This range of objects would look equally good in a variety of interiors.

YARN REQUIREMENTS – Appleton's crewel wool		
	box top + card holder	spectacle case
721	1 skein	1 skein
696	1 skein	1 skein
926	1 skein	1 skein
692	2 skeins	3 skeins
643	1 skein	1 skein
998	2 skeins	3 skeins
background 725	½ hank	1 hank

DRESSING TABLE SET

*Dressing table set comprising five matching objects:
a jewellery cushion, a mirror frame, a drawstring
bag, a round trinket box and a small mat.*

THE JEWELLERY CUSHION

- **You will need** *a 25 cm (10 in) square of size 18 interlock mono canvas*
- *DMC Médicis wools and perlé nr 5 in the shades and quantities given on page 75*
- *1 needle size 24*

The chart for the cushion reproduced below appears on the opposite page. It shows a quarter section of the design and does not include the central monogram. Make up your own initials, using the alphabet shown on page 106. Alternatively, you can keep the centre plain.

Measure 5 cm (2 in) from the edge of the canvas and start stitching the outline of a corner motif, as indicated on the chart.

Work all the outlines in continental tent stitch. Then fill in the motifs and backgrounds, using diagonal tent stitch.

A single row of long-legged cross stitch frames the design. **Three strands** of Médicis wool were used throughout. The details were worked in **one strand** of perlé nr 5.

Stretch and starch the completed piece and make up, following the instructions on page 118.

Jewellery cushion. Overall size: 21 x 21 cm (8.5 x 8.5 in).

Chart for jewellery cushion

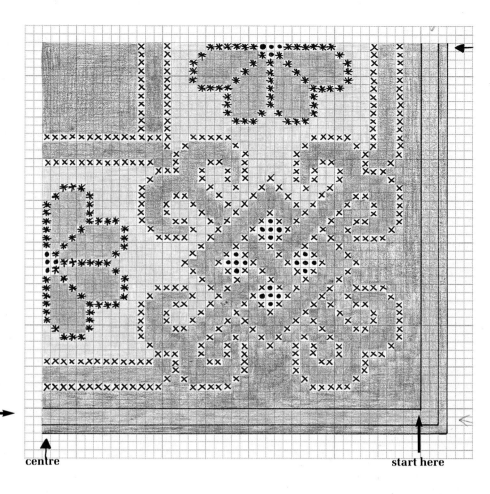

long-legged
cross stitch

centre

start here

YARN REQUIREMENTS
DMC Médicis wool

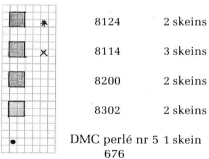

✳	8124	2 skeins
✗	8114	3 skeins
	8200	2 skeins
	8302	2 skeins
●	DMC perlé nr 5 1 skein 676	

COLOUR GUIDE – DMC Médicis wool

8114   8200   8302   8124   DMC
                                perlé nr 5
                                676

Mirror frame. Overall size: 25 x 25 cm (10 x 10 in).

MIRROR FRAME & DRAWSTRING BAG

- **You will need for the mirror frame:**
- *a 35 cm (14 in) square of size 14 interlock mono canvas*
- *DMC Médicis wools and perlé nr 5 in the shades and quantities given below*
- *1 needle size 22*
- *1 15 cm (6 in) square mirror tile*
- *embroidery frame (optional)*

- **For the bag:**
- *a 20 x 50 cm (8 x 20 in) oblong of size 14 interlock canvas*
- *DMC Médicis wools and perlé nr 5 in the shades and quantities given below*
- *1 needle size 22*

When the embroidery is complete, stretch and starch the pieces. Better let a professional framer assemble the mirror, which can be free-standing on a strut, as in the example illustrated here, or finished to hang on the bedroom wall.

To make up the bag, follow the instructions on page 125.

The chart reproduced on page 78 will enable you to work the mirror frame or the bag.

The working instructions are the same as for the jewellery cushion on page 74, except that you must use **five strands** of DMC Médicis wool and **two strands** of perlé nr 5.

Bag. Diameter of base 11 cm (4.5 in).

YARN REQUIREMENTS
DMC Médicis wool

			mirror	bag
	✳	8124	7 skeins	3 skeins
	✕	8114	7 skeins	4 skeins
		8200	6 skeins	2 skeins
		8302	4 skeins	2 skeins
•		DMC perlé nr 5 676	1 skein	1 skein

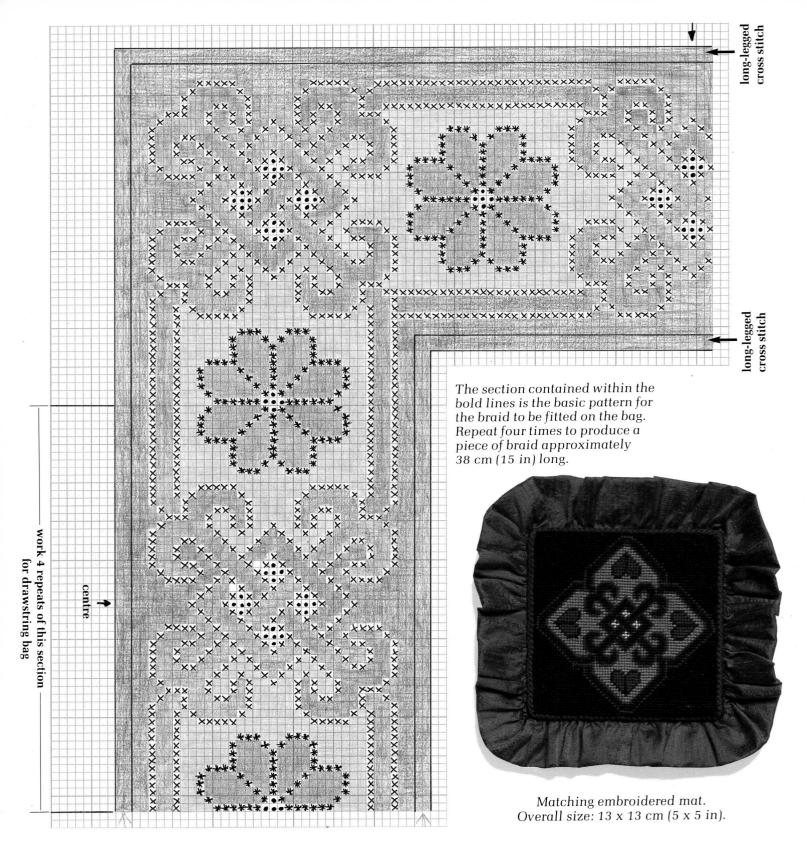

long-legged cross stitch

long-legged cross stitch

The section contained within the bold lines is the basic pattern for the braid to be fitted on the bag. Repeat four times to produce a piece of braid approximately 38 cm (15 in) long.

work 4 repeats of this section for drawstring bag

centre

Matching embroidered mat.
Overall size: 13 x 13 cm (5 x 5 in).

TRINKET BOX & MAT

- **You will need** *a 20 cm (8 in) square of size 18 interlock mono canvas*
- *DMC Médicis wools and perlé nr 5 in the shades and quantities given below*
- *1 needle size 24*

- *These requirements apply to either object, but to make the box, you will need to purchase a 9 cm (3.5 in) diameter ready-made wooden base.*

Right. Wooden trinket box with embroidered lid. Diameter: 9 cm (3.5 in).

YARN REQUIREMENTS
DMC Médicis wool
(mat or box top)

■	*	8124	1 skein
■	×	8114	1 skein
■		8200	2 skeins
■		8302	1 skein
	●	DMC perlé nr 5 676	1 skein

Trinket box and mat Fold the canvas into four to find the centre. The chart on the right shows one quarter of the design. Begin the embroidery from the centre, as marked on the chart.

Work all the outlines in continental tent stitch. Then fill in the motifs and backgrounds, using diagonal tent stitch. **Three strands** of Médicis wool were used throughout. The details were worked in **one strand** of perlé nr 5. Stretch and starch the completed pieces and make up the lid of the trinket box by following the manufacturer's instructions. To make up the mat, follow the instructions on page 125.

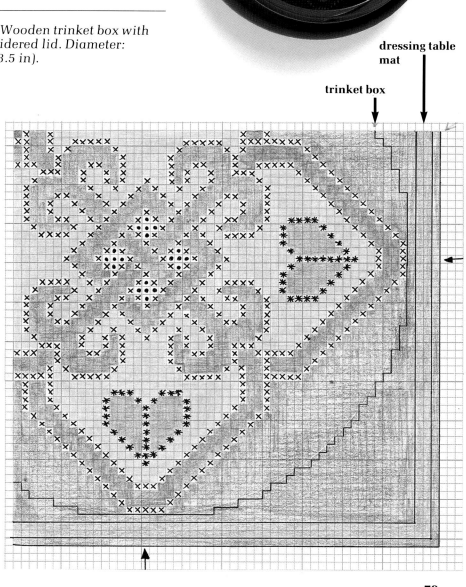

dressing table mat

trinket box

BARGELLO – A FEAST OF COLOURS

I have always been fascinated by bargello, its simplicity and the way in which it lends itself to filling awkward shapes. This form of embroidery was originally inspired by the moving motions of the fire and was known as 'flame stitch'. Bargello is now often used in a very structured way with the 'flames' moving regularly, in a predetermined pattern. I prefer the free-hand version and it is this method I have used for the projects in this series. Similar patterns are also found on traditional marbled papers, as can be observed in the endpapers of the nineteenth-century book illustrated on the left.

Nineteenth-century edition of The Natural History of Selborne *with comb-marbled endpapers.*

A detail from a panel covered in seventeenth-century flame stitch.

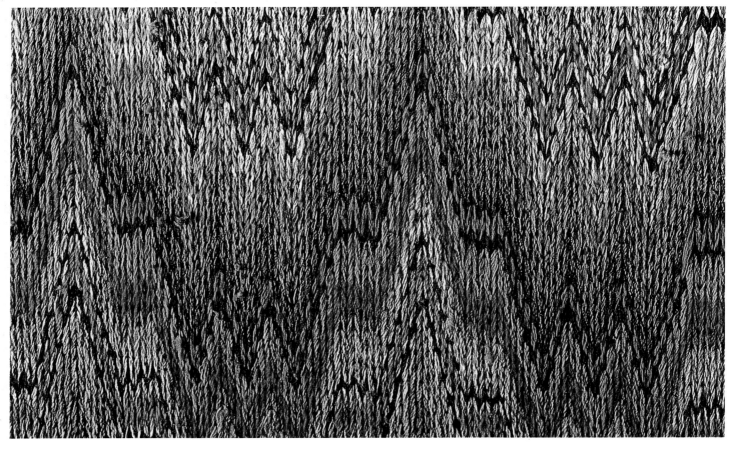

*Victorian nursing chair upholstered with bargello
embroidery. Matching curtain ties – the cushion was worked in
a different colourway.*

EMBROIDERED CHAIR SEAT WITH MATCHING CURTAIN TIE-BACKS

- **You will need** *For the chair: a piece of size 18 interlock mono canvas allowing for a 10 cm (4 in) margin outside the embroidered area (see below)*
- *Appleton's crewel wool in the shades and quantities given below*
- *1 needle size 22*
- *embroidery frame*

- *For the curtain ties (pair): a 70 x 40 cm (28 x 16 in) oblong of size 18 interlock mono canvas*
- *Other requirements as specified above*

the cushion illustrated on page 87. The furnishing material used for mounting the cushion has an intricate striped design in a contrasting colour range. Yet by carefully choosing and blending the wools in the embroidery, an attractive piece was produced.

I have specified the colours of the particular yarns I used to produce

I like combining bargello with patterned fabrics and enjoy picking out the colours already present in the material and allowing them to determine the colour scheme for the embroidery. This needs some care to ensure a successful blending of the shades within the embroidery. It is also important that a heavily patterned fabric does not overwhelm the embroidery. A good example is

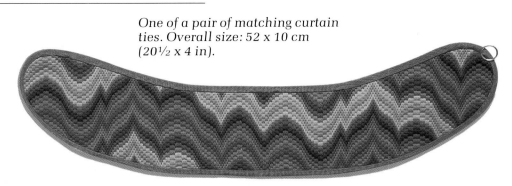

One of a pair of matching curtain ties. Overall size: 52 x 10 cm (20½ x 4 in).

the pieces in this section. Remember that these were chosen to complement a particular printed fabric, such as the curtains contained by the tie-backs. You should really devise a specific colour scheme to marry up with your own furnishings.

To achieve this, determine the three or four dominant colours in the fabric and match wools to these. Then choose a lighter and a darker shade for each. Take your time and arrange them side by side, stand back, and see how the colours interact.

The chair. You need to make a paper template of the chair seat you want to cover. If in doubt, consult a reputable upholsterer. Having established the shape and

YARN REQUIREMENTS – Appleton's crewel wool

golds	692	693	695
greens	332	334	336
mauves	932	933	934
reds	205	721	207

1 hank of each of the above produced the curtain tie-backs **and** the seat cover. Exact yarn quantities will be determined by the size of the seat to be covered.

COLOUR GUIDE – Appleton's crewel wool

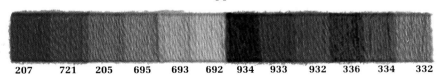

| 207 | 721 | 205 | 695 | 693 | 692 | 934 | 933 | 932 | 336 | 334 | 332 |

dimensions, make a paper template and draw the shape on to the canvas, using a waterproof pen.

Tie-backs. On page 121, you will find a pattern. Enlarge it as instructed. If the curtains are very full, you may have to increase the length of the ties. Check by cutting out a trial example in calico to see whether it fits. The pattern provided in the book explains how to increase the length of the ties, if necessary. Having established the size, draw the pattern twice on to the canvas, using a waterproof pen.

Overleaf you will find a chart of the embroidered design I have used for all the pieces in this section. The chart represents one of the darker lines. Begin stitching, using **three strands** of Appleton's crewel wool in one of the darker shades, from the left-hand side of the canvas on the line you have drawn. Follow the chart until you reach the end of the design. It probably will not span the whole width of the chair seat and you will need to repeat the pattern from the beginning. This is suggested by the dotted section on the chart.

As in the embroidered example shown under the chart, work this line right across the piece of canvas until you reach the line drawn on the opposite side.

Once this line has been worked, the whole piece of embroidery will follow naturally. On either side, work first the middle then the lighter shade. Repeat this process for the other colours.

As you approach the top or the bottom edge of the piece, you will find that some of the 'peaks' of the pattern cannot be completed.

Up till now you have always worked over four canvas threads, but in order to fill in the design up to the inked line, the stitches will have to decrease in length until you work over a single thread of the canvas, as you reach the edge of the embroidery. The narrower the piece the quicker this stage is reached. The tie-back is a good example.

When the embroidery is complete, stretch and starch the piece. In the case of the chair seat, hand over to the upholsterer. For the tie-backs, turn to page 121 for the making-up instructions.

Victorian nursing chair with embroidered seat. Size of seat: 56 x 56 cm (22 x 22 in)

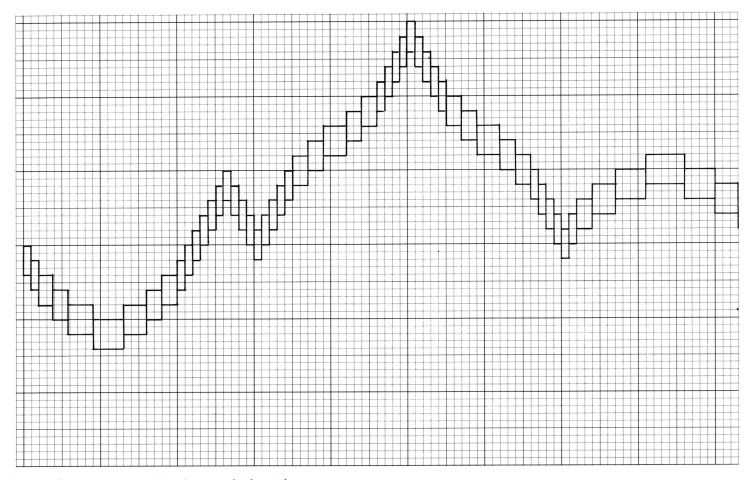

Start from this point and work towards the right.

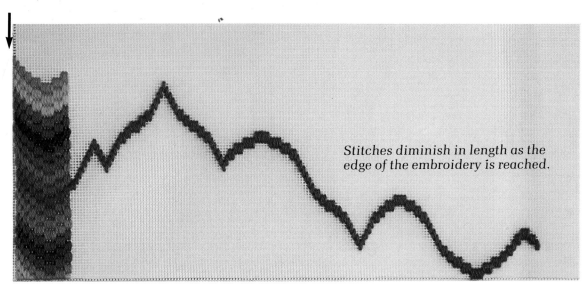

Stitches diminish in length as the edge of the embroidery is reached.

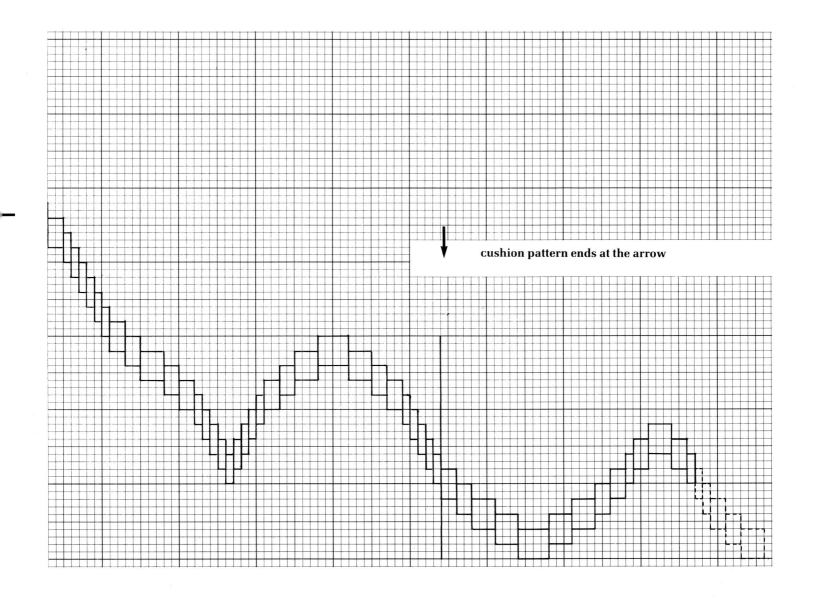

cushion pattern ends at the arrow

This chart shows the 'skeleton' of the piece of bargello.

THE BARGELLO CUSHION

- **You will need** *a 35 cm square (14 in) of size 18 interlock mono canvas*
- *Appleton's crewel wools in the shades and quantities given below*
- *1 needle size 22*
- *embroidery frame*

This cushion uses the same chart as the previous objects. (*See previous spread.*) Draw a line 5 cm (2 in) in from the left-hand edge of the canvas. Start the embroidery round about the middle of this line.

Begin work, using **three strands** of one of the darker shades of wool. Follow the chart until you reach the line marked. This will give a width of approximately 20 cm (8 in). The embroidered panel is square. Draw lines top and bottom to complete the 20 cm (8 in) square.

The working method is exactly the same as for the chair and the tie-backs.

Once the square had been filled completely, the edges were outlined with three rows of long-legged cross stitch, using the three darker shades.

Stretch and starch as before and refer to the making-up instructions on page 118.

YARN REQUIREMENTS – Appleton's crewel wool

blues	154	155	156
golds	693	695	696
reds	721	205	204

2 skeins of each of the above are needed to produce the cushion inset.

Right. Cushion with bargello inset panel. Overall size: 35 x 35 cm (14 x 14 in).

COLOUR GUIDE – Appleton's crewel wool

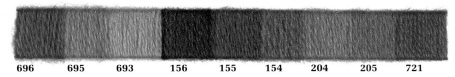

| 696 | 695 | 693 | 156 | 155 | 154 | 204 | 205 | 721 |

VARIATIONS ON A 16TH-CENTURY TAPESTRY

I was enchanted by the Sheldon tapestry, which is like a flower garden, lived in by fantastic animals. It is so complex that every time I see it, new details come to light.

A striking characteristic of the tapestry is the small size of the subjects in relation to the overall size of the piece itself. The plants and animals are crammed in over every available inch of the background. Strangely, it suggested a miniature to me. And therefore when I came to design a piece inspired by the tapestry, it ended up as a tiny panel. The flowers and insects as well as the border all appear in the tapestry, although I grouped them differently and adapted the design to be embroidered, as the original is woven. I retained the rich green background which forms such a striking feature of the original.

To use the same panel, without its border, as an inset on an evening bag, seemed a logical development. I was lucky enough to have already found a suitable antique clasp on which to mount the bag. It is quite difficult to find modern frames that are as attractive as the old ones, and searching antique shops is always a pleasure to me.

The Sheldon Tapestry. This remarkable piece of work was manufactured in England in the late 16th century. Originally made to be used as a tablecloth, it took as its subject the Expulsion from Paradise. The medallions contain vignettes of 'Justice', 'Providence', 'Charity' and other allegorical figures. The tapestry forms part of the collection at Sudeley Castle, Gloucestershire.

Square picture with embroidered inset panel, evening bag and miniature in a silver frame.

SQUARE PICTURE WITH EMBROIDERED INSET

- **You will need** *a 25 cm (10 in) square of size 18 interlock mono canvas*
- *DMC stranded cottons in the shades and quantities shown below*
- *1 needle size 22*
- *1 needle size 24*
- *embroidery frame*

Fold the canvas in four to find the centre. Mark it with a pencil. The motif occupying the centre square appears life-size on page 92. Trace it on to paper and fix the tracing on to a flat surface with masking tape. Lay the canvas over this tracing, aligning the centre marks. Trace the pattern over the canvas with a waterproof pen, except for the broken line which is to serve as a guide only.

Using the finer needle – size 24 – begin embroidering the flowers. Next to the drawing already mentioned, there is a partially worked panel which should help you.

Use all **six strands** of the stranded cotton throughout, except for the split back-stitch outlines to the flowers and the insects which use **two strands**.

The violets. The flowers are worked in long-and-short stitch (*see page 110*), using nrs 3740 and 3042. The leaves are worked in satin stitch (*see page 110*), using 936 and 734 (refer to the partially worked panel for guidance). The veins on the leaves and the stems are worked in split back stitch (*see page 109*), using 732. The violets are outlined using 839. The same shade is used to make three French knots (*see page 109*), in the centre of each flower.

The gold daisies on the right. The petals are worked in long-and-short stitch, using 680 and 632. The leaves are worked in satin stitch in 734 and the stems and veins are worked in split back stitch, using 732. In the centre of each flower there is a ring of French knots worked in 355 which is filled in with a cluster of French knots in 839. The petals are outlined in split back stitch, using 839.

The white columbine. The petals are worked in long-and-short stitch, using 3033. The hanging stamens are split back stitch, using **two strands** of 680. Each stamen ends with a French knot. The stems are worked in split back stitch, using 731. The flower petals are outlined in split back stitch in 422.

YARN REQUIREMENTS – DMC stranded cotton

	picture	bag (page 95)		picture	bag (page 95)
500	3 skeins	3 skeins	732	1 skein	1 skein
839	2 skeins	1 skein	731	1 skein	1 skein
422	2 skeins	1 skein	936	1 skein	1 skein
355	1 skein	1 skein	3033	1 skein	1 skein
3740	1 skein	1 skein	680	1 skein	1 skein
3042	1 skein	1 skein	632	1 skein	1 skein
734	1 skein	1 skein	370	1 skein	1 skein

COLOUR GUIDE – DMC stranded cotton

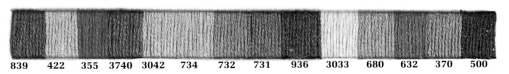

839 422 355 3740 3042 734 732 731 936 3033 680 632 370 500

See below for a key to the symbols used for the border and insect motifs charted opposite.

SYMBOLS TO CHART
DMC stranded cotton

●	355
✕	839
╲	3740
·	370
=	680
○	632

All blank squares
within border   422

Insect outlines   370

This drawing is shown life-size. The broken line is a guideline only.

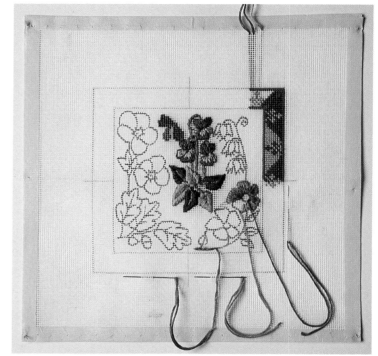

Partially worked example, showing how the long-and-short stitch technique is used to blend the colours within the flower motifs.

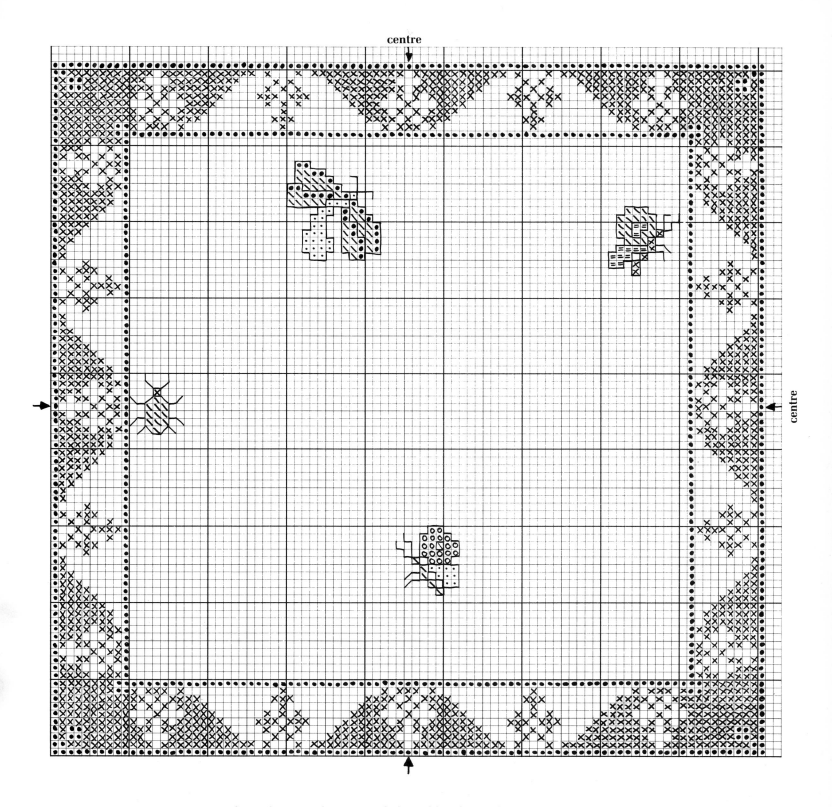

centre

centre

Chart showing the counted-thread border and insect motifs.

The red and white anemone on the left. The flower petals are worked in long-and-short stitch, using 3033 and 355. The centre of each flower has a single row of long-and-short stitch, using 680, and is finished with three French knots, using 839. The leaf is worked in satin stitch, using 732. The stems and veins are in split back stitch in 734.

The oak leaves and acorns. The acorns are worked in long-and-short stitch, using 422, and their cups are worked in tent stitch, using 370. The leaves are worked in long-and-short stitch in 936 and 731. The stems and veins, and the outlines to the acorn cups are in split back stitch, using 839.

Refer once again to the drawing on page 92. The broken line framing the motif is there to guide you, but you must **count** 71 canvas threads in both directions to enable you to position the border accurately. Draw a pencil line around this square. Count a further ten threads out in each direction and draw a second pencil line which will form the outer edge of the border.

The next step is to work the insects: turn to the chart on page 93. You will find it easier to use a thicker needle – nr 22 – for the rest of the work. The insects are worked in continental tent stitch (see page 109). You will note from the picture and from the partly worked example that I have worked the tent stitch in the opposite direction to that used for the background. This was deliberate in order to emphasize these tiny elements. The outlines are left until the green background is complete.

Start the border using the size 22 needle and following the chart. Use continental tent stitch throughout.

Fill the background, in green – nr 500 – using diagonal tent stitch (see page 109) and a size 22 needle. As you progress towards the flowers, make sure to tuck your stitches *under* the long-and-short stitch and the split back-stitch outlines of the flowers and leaves. This is to ensure that the white canvas does not show.

Finally, work the back-stitch outlines to the insects, using **two strands** of cotton.

Stretch and starch the finished piece. Hand over to a reputable framer to mount.

SILVER-FRAMED MINIATURE

I had a miniature silver frame and decided to use the left-over cotton to work a tiny picture to fit inside it. If you wish to do the same, you should first find a frame to ensure that the chosen subject will fit and to determine the amount of background required.

Select your favourite flower out of the master drawing on page 92. Transfer the motif on to a scrap of size 18 canvas, as instructed before. Follow the instructions for the embroidery and fill in the background to fit the frame.

Stretch and starch as explained on page 113. Mount as per frame-manufacturers' instructions.

Silver-framed miniature, 9 cm (3½ in) high.

EVENING BAG

- **You will need** *a 25 cm square (10 in) square of size 18 interlock mono canvas*
- *DMC stranded cottons in the shades and quantities given on page 90*
- *1 needle size 22*
- *1 needle size 24*
- *embroidery frame*
- *1 bag clasp*

Yarn requirements for the bag appear on page 90. These are specific to this size of bag which depends on that of the clasp.

The bag illustrated opposite is made up of the same panel as the square picture on page 91, except for the border which was omitted. I have also extended the green background, top and bottom, to turn the square into an upright shape, which fits the bag better.

It is impossible to give specific measurements for the finished panel, as this will be determined by the size of clasp, and therefore of bag, that you want to produce.

It is essential to stretch and starch this piece carefully, so that the bag does not twist and distort when made up.

Suggested making-up instructions appear on page 126, but you may need to adapt them to fit the purchased clasp.

Evening bag with inset embroidered panel. Overall size: 19 x 15 cm (7½ x 6 in).

PATCHWORK

Like most people interested in needlework in all its forms, I have a partially completed patchwork bedspread which was begun with great enthusiasm several years ago and has since languished in a drawer. But I know that 'one day' it will be finished to become a treasured family heirloom. One of the wonderful things about patchwork is that old and new fabrics can be mixed so that individual pieces are almost like extracts from a scrap book – bringing back memories of children's dresses and of fabrics used in our previous home. Yet the colours and patterns marry up to form a new piece.

As I was about to finish this book, it occurred to me that the various designs and patterns used could be worked into octagons, arranged side by side to simulate real patchwork. I discovered that patterns, which at first seemed disparate, sat quite happily next to each other.

While I was working on the project, my eyes alighted on my favourite needlepoint pincushion – one of my very first designs – and I decided to include it with the project. It is reproduced below and you will find a chart for it on page 105.

Modern hand-made patchwork cushion in a fresh and cool combination of colours.

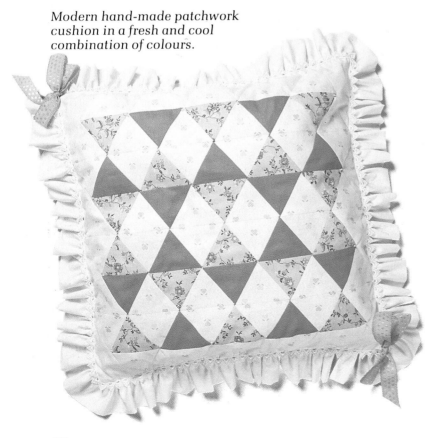

My old pincushion – still one of my favourite pieces. Overall size: 12 x 12 cm (4.5 x 4.5 in).

The finished embroidered 'patchwork' cushion with its nine octagons and bargello border.

PATCHWORK CUSHION

- **You will need** *a 45 x 45 cm (18 x 18 in) square of size 14 interlock mono canvas*
- *a selection of yarns as stipulated with each individual chart or according to taste*
- *1 needle size 22*
- *embroidery frame*

All nine octagons have been charted over the next few pages. With each chart you will find a list of the colours used. When I worked the cushion, I was able to use up many left-over yarns from the original projects. I therefore did not include quantities as I

would like to encourage you to use up thread you already have, as you would do with fabrics on a real patchwork cushion. It is easy to produce a larger cushion by adding an extra octagon in each direction, to end up with sixteen. The bargello border comes from

the Tudor Collection (*see* page 14 for general instructions). The corner is different here and the chart below shows you how to work it.

Fold the canvas into four to find the centre and begin by working

Chart showing 'skeleton' octagons and detail of border. The border is finished off with two rows of long-legged cross stitch.

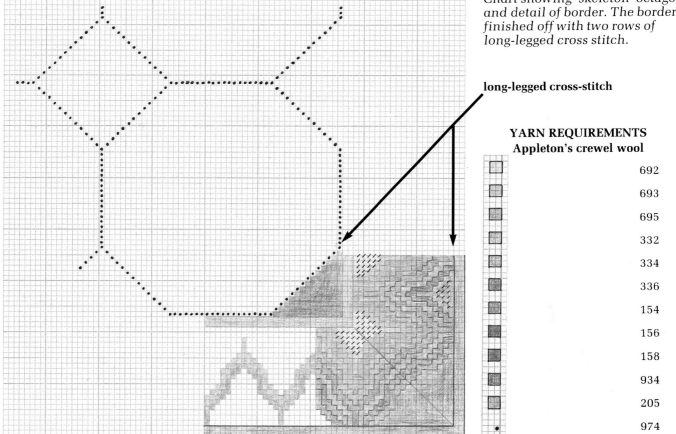

long-legged cross-stitch

YARN REQUIREMENTS
Appleton's crewel wool

	692
	693
	695
	332
	334
	336
	154
	156
	158
	934
	205
	974

Patchwork cushion. Overall size:
40 x 40 cm (16 x 16 in).

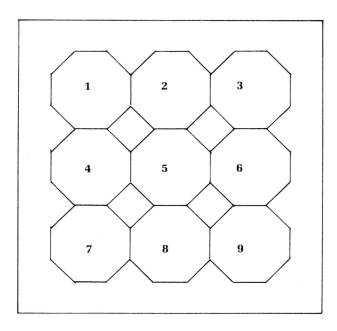

This is the order in which the nine octagons appear on the cushion and will be charted over the ensuing pages.

the outline to the central octagon, using continental tent stitch and **three strands** of Appleton's crewel wool, nr 974. The diagram opposite and the chart on the previous page will show you how. Follow each chart in turn to complete all nine octagons. Refer to the chapters from which the pieces are drawn for working instructions. Remember that some of the original projects were worked on a different gauge of canvas; if the number of strands to be used in the octagons has now changed, this is specified next to the small charts.

FIRST OCTAGON

Tudor Collection. See page 11. The actual piece was worked on size 14 canvas too; you can therefore follow original instructions exactly.

YARN REQUIREMENTS
Appleton's crewel wool

flower	leaves & stems
203	332
204	334
205	336
207	

background: 692

SECOND OCTAGON

Bargello. *See page 83. The original piece was worked on size 18 canvas.* Here you must use **four strands** of wool.

YARN REQUIREMENTS
Appleton's crewel wool

932	332
933	334
934	336
692	205
693	721
695	207

The first line marked on the chart is worked in 693

THIRD OCTAGON

Tunisian Images. *See page 32 and follow original instructions.*

YARN REQUIREMENTS
Appleton's crewel wool

●		974
▢		206
✕		154
·		931
⁄.		693
∧		343
=	DMC perlé nr 3	739

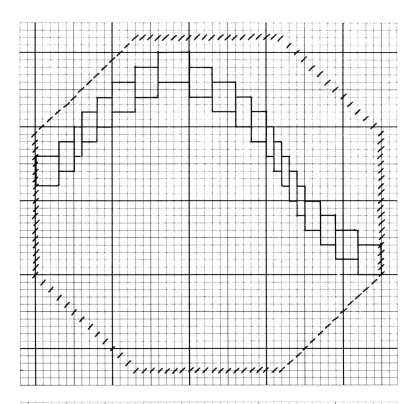

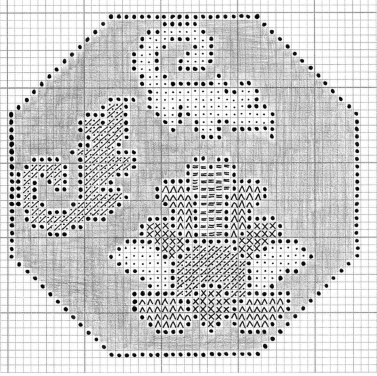

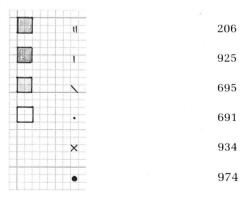

FOURTH OCTAGON

Victorian Pansies. See page 22.
The original was worked on size
18 canvas. Here you must use
nine strands of stranded cotton
(one and a half thicknesses of the
yarn as supplied) and **three
strands** of Appleton's wool.

YARN REQUIREMENTS
DMC stranded cotton

■	3371			783
	520		○	676
	522			677
✕	315		▽	3041
—	316		|	3042
•	778		●	974 (Appleton's)

background: Appleton's crewel wool 933

FIFTH OCTAGON

Colours from the Orient. See
page 56 and follow original
instructions.

YARN REQUIREMENTS
Appleton's crewel wool

▧	↿	206
▨	↾	925
☐	\	695
☐		691
	✕	934
	●	974

SIXTH OCTAGON

The Tudor Collection. *See* page 11 and follow original instructions.

YARN REQUIREMENTS
Appleton's crewel wool

strawberries	leaves & stems
695	334
207	332

background: 692 and 156

SEVENTH OCTAGON

This design is based on the pincushion shown on page 96. Follow instructions on page 105, but using **three strands** of Appleton's crewel wool.

YARN REQUIREMENTS
Appleton's crewel wool

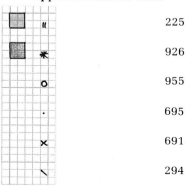

◨	ıı	225
◨	✳	926
	○	955
	·	695
	✕	691
	＼	294

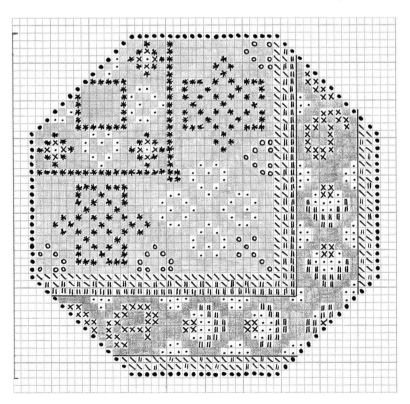

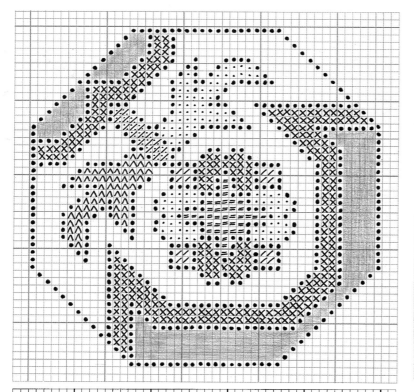

EIGHTH OCTAGON

Tunisian Images. See page 32 and follow original instructions.

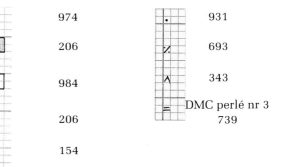

YARN REQUIREMENTS
Appleton's crewel wool

•	974	.	931	
☐	206	╱	693	
☐	984	∧	343	
╱	206	=	DMC perlé nr 3 739	
×	154			

NINTH OCTAGON

Bargello. See page 83 but use **four strands** of Appleton's wool.

Stretch and starch the finished piece and make up, using the instructions on page 118.

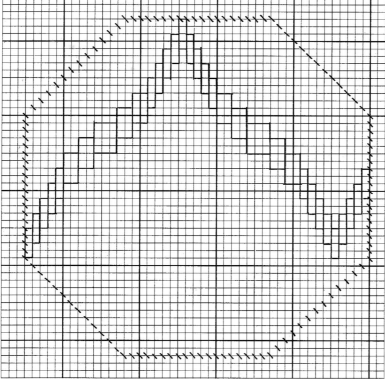

YARN REQUIREMENTS
Appleton's crewel wool

332	934
334	205
336	721
932	207
933	

The first line marked on the chart is worked in 205

THE PINCUSHION

- **You will need** *a 20 x 20 cm (8 x 8 in) square of size 18 interlock mono canvas*
- *Appleton's crewel wools in the shades and quantities given below*
- *1 needle size 22*
- *embroidery frame (optional)*

Fold the piece of canvas to find the centre and begin by working the blue square in the middle. Work the motifs in continental tent stitch and the backgrounds in diagonal tent stitch.

Use **two strands** of Appleton's crewel wool throughout.

Stretch and starch the finished piece and back with fabric. I made a twisted cord (see page 115) with the left-over wool and slip-stitched it over the seam, making a loop at each corner.

Finished pincushion. Overall size: 12 x 12 cm (4.5 x 4.5 in).

YARN REQUIREMENTS
Appleton's crewel wool

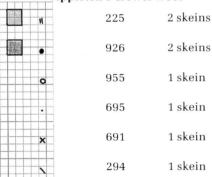

◫	ΙΙ	225	2 skeins
◫	●	926	2 skeins
	o	955	1 skein
	·	695	1 skein
	×	691	1 skein
	＼	294	1 skein

COLOUR GUIDE – Appleton's crewel wool

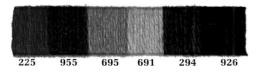

| 225 | 955 | 695 | 691 | 294 | 926 |

Chart for pincushion

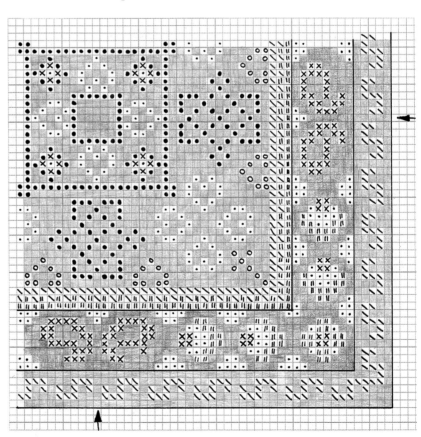

centre

ALPHABETS & MONOGRAMS

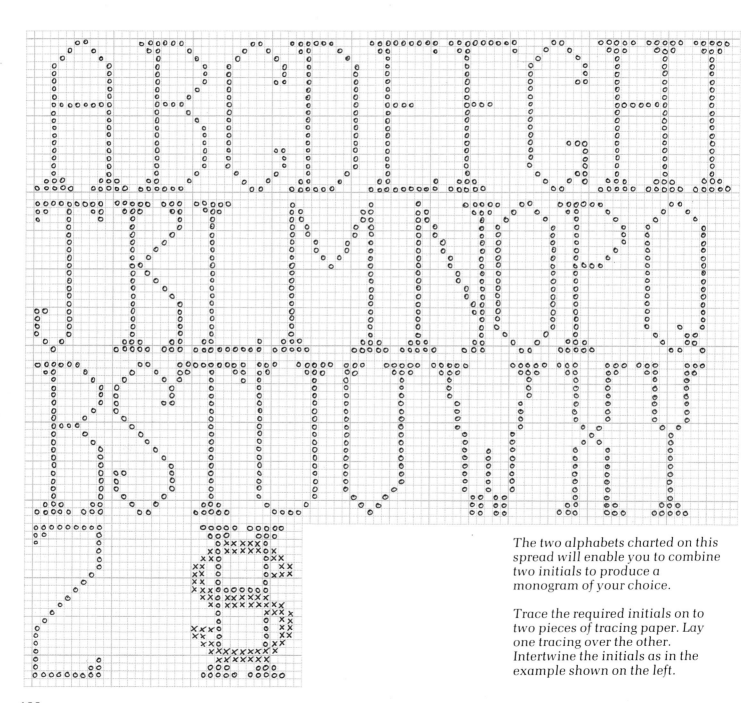

The two alphabets charted on this spread will enable you to combine two initials to produce a monogram of your choice.

Trace the required initials on to two pieces of tracing paper. Lay one tracing over the other. Intertwine the initials as in the example shown on the left.

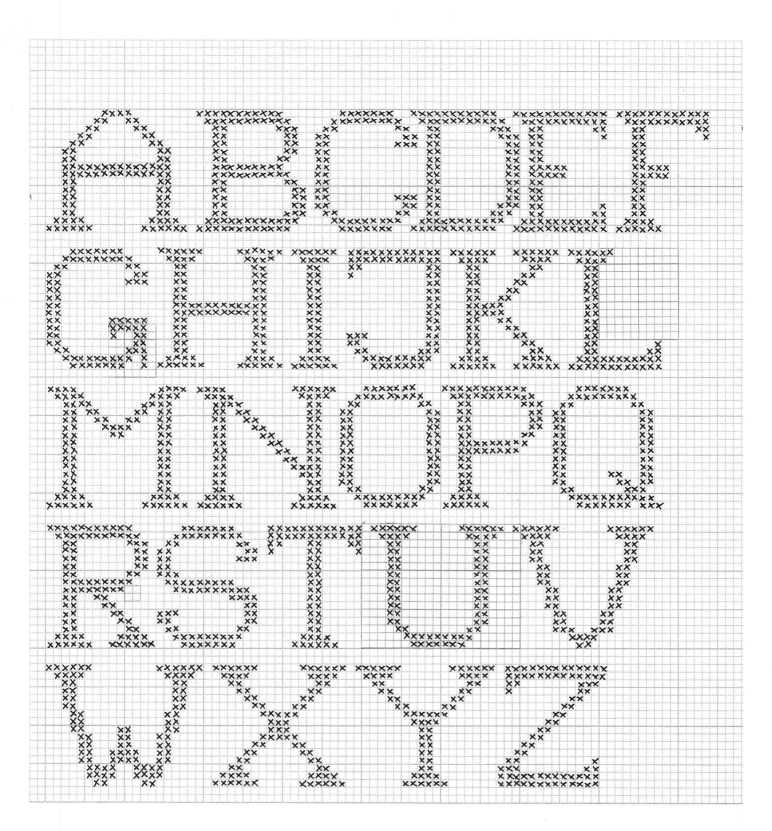

These two alphabets and the
numerals will enable you to
complete the wedding ring
pillow illustrated on page 25.

GLOSSARY OF STITCHES

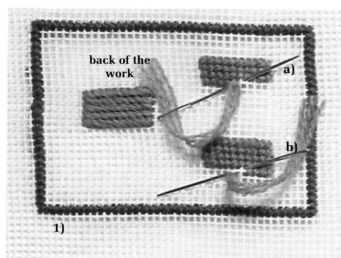

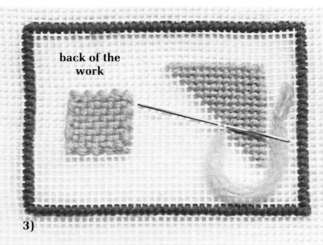

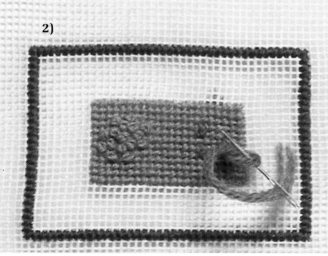

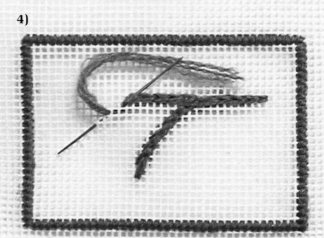

1) Continental tent stitch
   a) continental tent stitch worked from left to right
   b) continental tent stitch worked from right to left

2) French knots
   French knots do not sit well on bare canvas. First cover the canvas with tent stitch, then wind the yarn once around the needle and, keeping a gentle tension on the free end of the thread, push the needle down between the next tent stitches.

3) Diagonal tent stitch
   Also known as basketweave stitch.

4) Split back stitch
   Worked in the same way as ordinary back stitch, except that the stitches overlap and each succeeding stitch is worked **through** the previous one, splitting the threads.

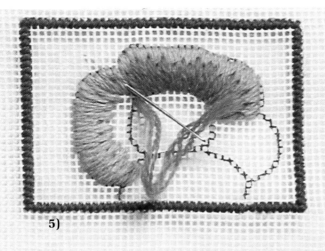

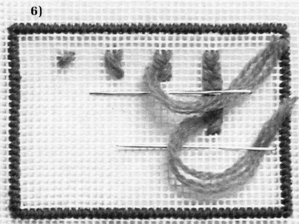

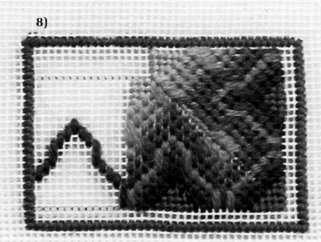

5) Long-and-short stitch

Ensure that you use every canvas hole around the edge of the flower or leaf and overlap the stitches in the centre to follow the shape on the canvas. The second layer of stitches is worked into the first, splitting the threads to ensure that the colours blend.

6) Long-legged cross stitch

This stitch covers two canvas threads and is worked two threads forward and two threads backward to give a 'braided' effect.

7) Satin stitch

Long smooth stitches fill the lines of the design. You will need to work more than once into each hole in the centre of the leaf motif.

8) Bargello or flame stitch

Detail from the border used in the Tudor Collection. Shows the corner and the tent-stitch infills.

EQUIPMENT & MATERIALS

THREADS

There is a variety of yarns and threads available on the market and all needlepoint workers seem to have their own particular favourites. I prefer working with Appleton's crewel wool, partly because their large and carefully graded colour range suit my work, but also because I like the smoothness of the yarn itself. To vary texture, I quite often mix cotton with wool within one piece. I find that embroidering part of the motif in DMC perlé, for instance, and the background in wool, makes the motif appear almost jewel-like. I have also used Paterna Persian yarn and DMC Médicis wool, yet I always come back to my perennial favourites. Crewel wool is a fine, twisted two-ply yarn which may be used singly or as two or more strands in the needle. I find it easier to work with several thin strands in the needle than with a single thick thread. When several strands are used in this way, the wool lies flat and covers the entire area of the canvas perfectly. If you stitch very tightly, and some of the canvas shows through the embroidery (especially if you work with dark thread over white canvas) try adding an extra strand of crewel wool to your needleful. Appleton's crewel wools are widely available in many countries and can be ordered from various suppliers. The international list at the end of this book should convince you of this. If you are having difficulties, however, and prefer to look for alternatives to Appleton's crewel wools, note that a colour guide has been included with each project. This will help you to match an alternative yarn. I have also included a conversion chart to DMC Médicis wool below for the colours I have used in this book. Remember, however, that the conversions are approximate and that differences are bound to happen. This is unimportant so long as the final result is pleasing to the eye. Note that some DMC shades are offered more than once as an alternative to separate Appleton's colours. This is inevitable as the DMC Médicis range is more limited, but it should not constitute a problem as they do not appear together within one project.

Appleton's	Médicis	Appleton's	Médicis	Appleton's	Médicis
154	8214	294	8414	866	8126
155	8202	332	8405	882	ECRU
156	8203	334	8411	925	8207
158	8201	336	8422	926	8206
203	8111	343	8412	931	8119
204	8164	643	8407	932	8122
205	8166	691	8502	933	8136
206	8168	692	8314	934	8124
207	8114	693	8313	955	8610
221	8225	695	8303	974	8308
222	8224	696	8324	976	8307
223	8223	721	8168	984	8502
224	8107	725	8114	998	8500
225	8221	749	8205		

If the instructions in the book state **two strands** *of Appleton's, substitute* **three strands** *of DMC Médicis wool; or* **five strands** *of Médicis for* **three strands** *of Appleton's.*

CANVAS

Canvas is available in two main types: single-thread or mono canvas and double-thread or Penelope canvas. Single-thread canvas is easier to use and is also available as interlock mono canvas. This is the one I use. In this type the threads along the length are in fact double threads, twisted together to hold the cross threads firmly in place. This produces a more stable canvas that does not distort so readily. It should always be used for working designs including long stitches when it is easy to pull loose canvas threads together and make holes in the work. The only disadvantage with interlock mono canvas is that it only comes in white. Care needs to be taken not to stitch too tightly to avoid the canvas showing through the work.

NEEDLES

A tapestry needle has a blunt end which slips easily through the canvas mesh without catching. The size required will vary according to the number of strands of wool you are using. I tend to use a fairly fine needle, but you should use one you feel comfortable with. Needles are nickel-plated or gold-plated. Gold-plated needles have only recently become available. They are much smoother than the former and I always find them a pleasure to use.

EMBROIDERY FRAMES

To use an embroidery frame or not for canvas work embroidery is, I think, a matter of personal preference. You should do what you feel comfortable with. I recommend the use of a frame for any design which involves long stitches or which needs careful counting from a chart. I often work the motifs in a frame, then complete the backgrounds in my hand. If you work in the hand, you should roll the canvas rather than crunch it up and, of course, you will need to stretch the finished piece carefully as it distorts more than when worked on a frame.

Among the many types of frames available, choose one to fit your budget and that you feel most comfortable with. Try to borrow different ones from friends before deciding what to buy.

Do not use an embroidery loop, unless you have one big enough to contain the entire work surface. Where canvas has been stretched tightly between the rings, it will become distorted and if this distortion is then worked over, there will be a shadow in the work which often remains, after stretching.

STRETCHING & STARCHING EMBROIDERY

It is in the nature of canvas work to distort, especially when working in tent stitch. It is therefore vital to stretch and starch the finished piece to ensure that it is square. The starch also protects the back of the embroidery and will prolong its life.

- **You will need** *a large, flat, clean board (chipboard is ideal)*
- *a sheet of dressmaker's graph paper*
- *1 inch nails (enough to go round the edges of the piece at no more than 2 cm (¾ in) apart*
- *a hammer*
- *cold water starch (most easily available as wallpaper adhesive. Check that it does not contain plasticiser or other additives). I use a brand called Lap which is widely available*
- *masking tape*
- *a kitchen palette knife*

Cover the board with the sheet of squared-up paper and stick it down with masking tape. Place the embroidery, right side down, on top of the graph paper. You will be able to see the squares on the paper through the unstitched margins of the canvas. Begin nailing down in one corner about 5 cm (2 in) away from the embroidery. Hammer the nails just enough to hold the cloth firmly to the board. Follow one line of holes in the canvas and nail into every second intersection of a line in the paper. It is important to keep the nails no more than 2 cm (¾ in) apart or the embroidery will acquire a scalloped edge. When you have completed the first side, go back to the corner and repeat for the side at right angle to it. Draw a pencil line on the canvas from the last nail on each side to cross at the opposite corner to the one you started from. Work out where this corner should go in relation to the squares on the graph paper. Pull out the embroidery, nail this last corner and the two other sides.

If your work is badly distorted, it will help at this stage to dampen the embroidery. The embroidery should now be perfectly square. Mix a small quantity of starch paste to the consistency of soft butter and, using the palette knife, spread it evenly but sparingly over the back of the embroidery. Try not to let the starch go over the edges of the embroidery as it will stick the work to the paper which will tear when you remove the embroidery and you will have to change it to use the board again.

Allow to dry **completely.** Remove the nails and turn the embroidery over. You should find that not only is it perfectly square (the starch will ensure that it remains so) but also that the tension of the stitches will appear more even. I have dealt with stretching in some detail because I really think it is most important if you are to produce a finished piece you will always be proud of.

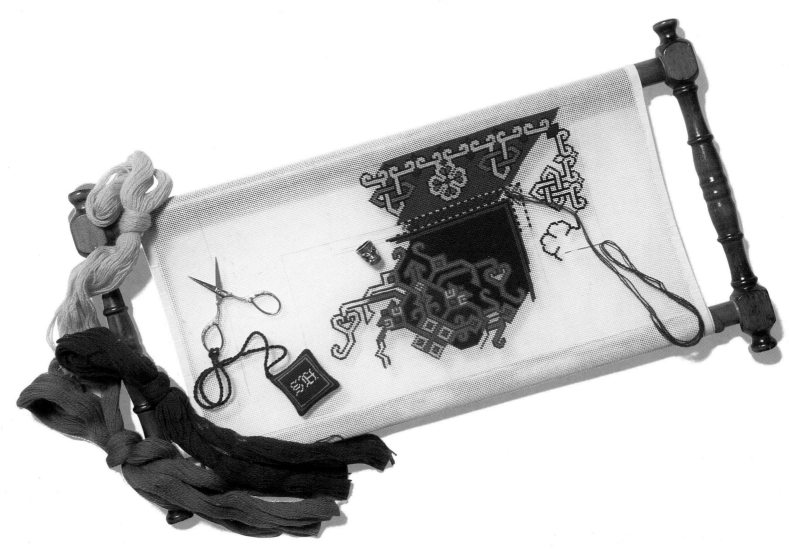

Having spent a great deal of time producing a piece of fine embroidery, it is important to show it off to best advantage. Even a relatively small amount of needlepoint can be made to look spectacular by mounting it on to a piece of carefully chosen fabric. Tassels, matching or contrasting piping are all devices which will contribute to making the work look professional and lend it long-lasting appeal.

INSTRUCTIONS FOR MAKING-UP

Interior design suppliers and furnishing shops stock a good range of trimmings but you may prefer to make your own. By using embroidery yarns to make tassels, for instance, a perfect colour match can be achieved. It is also a great deal cheaper – good quality trimmings tend to be rather expensive. Tassels, as used on the bolster, on page 61 may look intricate but they are quite easy and fun to make. Matching cords are even simpler to produce. Here again you can match the colours and textures of your work.

TASSELS

To make a simple tassel cut lengths of yarn to just over twice the finished length of the tassel. Tie them together firmly in the middle and fold the bundle in half. Use the ends of the tie to fix the tassel on to a piece of cord or a cushion corner.

To make larger and more intricate tassels, like the ones on the bolster, I used a large wooden bead (obtainable from most craft shops). Before tying off the head of the tassel, thread the bead on to some of the inner threads and bring the rest over the bead to cover it completely. Bind the threads together firmly below the head. You can then add decorative stitchery over the head of the tassel, as shown in the diagram left, by winding yarn around some of the outer threads of the tassel.

TWISTED OR MONK'S CORD

This is a simple but effective cord. I have used it to make the ties on the needle books, the drawstring on the bag shown on page 77, the corded edging on the small pincushions, the cords on the scissor and key keepers and the strap for the bag on page 60.

Decide how long and how thick you want the finished cord to be. You will require enough strands to make half the desired thickness. They should be three times the desired length. Tie a knot at both ends. Get someone to hold firmly to one end or secure it to a doorknob. Twist the other end clockwise until the yarn begins to double back on itself when you let the tension off slightly. Fold in half, let go of the centre point gradually, holding the two ends together. Tie the ends. If you need to cut the cord, make sure the ends are knotted or they will unravel. If you require a thicker cord, you can start with a long length, twisting and folding it twice.

MAKING-UP CUSHIONS

I prefer to make my cushions without a zip as I find these unsightly and if I need to remove the cover for cleaning, unpicking the hand-stitched side seems a small price to pay. If you decide to have a zip, simply cut the back panel of the cushion 5 cm (2 in) larger in one dimension, fold the cloth in half and cut along the fold. Use a zip 7.5 cm (3 in) shorter than the width of the finished cushion. Place the two back pieces right sides together and make a seam at each end, leaving a suitable opening to fit the zip. Taking 2.5 cm (1 in) turnings, sew in the zip. You can now treat this panel as one piece and complete the cushion according to your favourite method.

I prefer to hand-stitch plain piped cushions because I think that the end result is better. Having spent all that time on the embroidery, it is well worth the extra effort to obtain a really good finish. It is very difficult to machine-pipe exactly to the edge of the canvas work and you'll have more control doing it by hand.

Furthermore if you follow the method described on the right-hand page, you will not have to turn your cushion inside out to stitch it and then crumple it up to get the right side out. I use button thread to stitch with because it is strong enough to pull the stitches tightly, without breaking.

PLAIN PIPED CUSHION

(Large cushion from the Tudor Collection shown on page 8.)

- **You will need** *50 cm (20 in) of furnishing fabric*
- *piping cord nr 3*
- *cushion pad about 5 cm (2 in) larger than the finished cushion*
- *button thread for hand sewing*

Cut a square of furnishing fabric, 5 cm (2 in) larger than the finished area of embroidery. To make the piping, cut enough bias strips 4 cm (1.5 in) wide to go round the cushion. It is important that these strips are on the true bias of the fabric and are therefore cut at a 45 angle *see diagram 1).*

Stitch together enough bias strips to make the required length, *see diagram 2).* Fold the strip in half and, using the piping foot of your sewing machine, stitch the cord into the folded bias.

Trim the unstitched canvas edge within 2 cm (¾ in) of the embroidery, clipping each corner. Turn the edge under and catch down the unstitched canvas to the wrong side of the embroidery, using a herringbone stitch *see diagram 3).* Now you are ready to attach the prepared piping. Find the centre point of the edge that will be the bottom of the cushion and mark it with a pin. Leave an end of piping hanging loose to make a join at this point later. Stitch the piping to the embroidery, using slip stitches, *see diagram 4).* Make all your stitches into the tube of the piping to keep it taut against the edge of the embroidery. If you pull the

thread tightly, you will find that the stitches disappear into the edge of the embroidery. Clip the seam allowance of the piping cord at each corner.

To make a neat join in the piping lay one open end over the other. Cut away the excess, leaving a 1.25 cm (½ in) seam allowance at each end. Machine or hand-stitch.

Trim the two ends of the cord so that they butt up to each other and insert them back into the tube of the piping. Finish attaching the piping to the embroidery across the join. Turn the work over and lay the backing fabric over the cushion. Turn in the edges to fit, trimming the corners. Pin, leaving an opening on one side to insert the cushion pad. Slip-stitch the back to the piping in the same way as you did for the front. Insert the cushion pad and sew up the opening. Give the finished cushion a good 'beating' to force the pad into the corners.

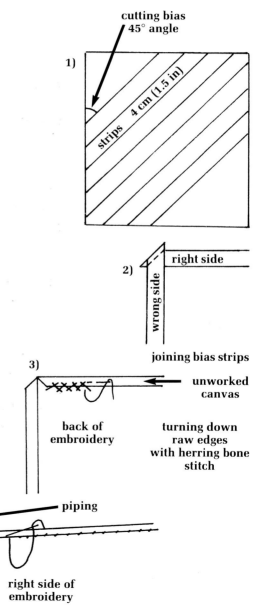

1) cutting bias 45° angle

strips 4 cm (1.5 in)

2) right side

wrong side

joining bias strips

3) back of embroidery

unworked canvas

turning down raw edges with herring bone stitch

4) piping

right side of embroidery

SET-IN CUSHION WITH MITRED CORNERS
– PIPE-EDGED OR FRILLED

*Velvet cushion from the Tudor Collection;
ivory and burgundy cushions, the wedding
ring pillow in Victorian Pansies; all four
cushions in Tunisian images; large cushion*
*and dressing table pillow in Magic carpet; the
cushion in Bargello – A Feast of Colours and
the one in Patchwork, all are made up
according to this method and either finish.*

- **You will need for pipe-edged version**
- *50 cm (20 in) of furnishing fabric*
- *piping cord nr 3*
- *cushion pad about 5 cm (2 in) larger than the finished cushion*

For frilled version
- *70 cm (28 in) of fabric fine enough to gather easily*
- *cushion pad as above*

The seam allowance throughout is 1.25 cm (½ in). Measure the embroidery and decide on the size that you would like the finished cushion to be. Subtract the embroidery measurement from the finished measurement, divide this by two and add on two seam allowances. This gives you the width for the border pieces. Using the cutting plans 1) or 2) shown opposite, cut all the pieces.

Trim the unstitched canvas edge within 2 cm (¾ in) of the embroidery and mark it with a pin. Pin the border panels to the embroidery, matching the centre points, and leaving the ends loose. Machine-stitch these seams using a piping foot. To avoid any unworked canvas showing on the finished cushion, take great care to stitch very close to the edge of the embroidery, the stitching of each side should meet at the corners through the same canvas hole of the embroidery. If you now fold the embroidery in half, diagonally, wrong sides together, you will find it easy to mitre the corners by stitching a line from the corner of the embroidery to the corner of the border panels – see diagram 3). Trim the excess cloth on this seam and clip the corners. Repeat, folding on the other diagonal, to mitre the other two corners.

Cushion with mitred corners and a frilled edge

1)

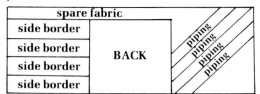

spare fabric		
side border	BACK	piping piping piping piping piping
side border		
side border		
side border		

cutting plan – piped version

2)

frill		
frill		
side border	BACK	
side border		
side border		
side border		

cutting plan – frilled version

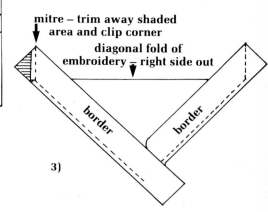

mitre – trim away shaded area and clip corner

diagonal fold of embroidery – right side out

border   border

3)

To make a piped cushion. Use a piping foot to make the piping and attach it to the outer edge of the front. Make a join at the bottom as for the plain piped cushion. Lay the back over the front, right sides together, and stitch, working tightly against the piping and leaving an opening at the bottom edge to insert the cushion pad. Turn right sides out, insert the pad and slip-stitch the opening to finish the cushion.

To make a frilled cushion. Seam the frill pieces together to form a continuous loop and fold this in half, right sides out. Run gathers along the raw edges and pull up to fit the outer edge of the cushion. Pin the frill to the edge of the front, spreading the gathers evenly, with the folded edges facing the centre of the cushion.

Stitch this seam. Pin the back to the front, right sides together. Stitch, leaving an opening to insert the cushion pad. Turn right sides out, insert the pad and slip-stitch the opening.

CUSHION WITH CORDED EDGE

(Pincushion in Patchwork chapter shown on page 105.)

- **You will need** *a piece of furnishing fabric measuring 5 cm (2 in) more than the embroidery*
- *a length of decorative cord at least 10 cm (4 in) longer than the edge of the finished cushion*
- *cushion pad about 5 cm (2 in) larger than the finished cushion*
- *button thread for hand sewing*

Trim the unstitched canvas edge within 2 cm (⅔ in) of the embroidery. Pin the embroidery and the fabric right sides together. Machine-stitch, using the piping foot, taking care to stitch very close to the embroidery. Leave an opening at the bottom to insert the cushion pad. Insert the cushion pad and slip-stitch the opening leaving a 2.5 cm (1 in) gap in the

centre. Tuck one end of the cord into this gap and catch each twist of the cord into the seam of the cushion, make sure you neither twist or untwist the cord as you stitch. When you have worked all round the cushion and reached the gap, trim off any excess cord. Tuck the end next to the first one, sew up the gap securely around the two ends.

The velvet cushion which belongs to The Tudor Collection and shown on page 15 has mitred corners and a corded edge.

PIPED CUSHION WITH INSET PANEL

The embroidery instructions for this project can be found on page 56.

- **You will need** *50 cm (20 in) of furnishing fabric (if a contrasting piping is required, a further 50 cm (20 in) of contrasting fabric must be purchased*
- *piping cord nr 3*
- *a cushion pad about 5 cm (2 in) larger than the finished cushion*
- *button thread for hand sewing*

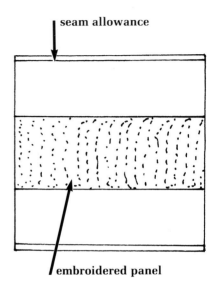

seam allowance

embroidered panel

Trim the unstitched canvas edge within 2 cm (⅔ in) of the embroidery. Measure the length of the panel and cut side panels which will make up the same measurements to produce a square, add 1.25 cm (½ in) for the seams (*see diagram opposite*).

Cut a square of fabric for the back of the cushion to the same measurements. Pin the embroidery, right sides together, with the two fabric panels. Machine-stitch very close to the embroidery, using the piping foot. Turn under the top and bottom edges of the embroidered panel and catch down to the back of the embroidery, using herringbone stitch – see diagram 3) on page 117. Turn in the seam allowance all around the side panels, the front of the cushion is now in one piece and you can follow the given instructions for the plain piped cushion on page 117.

TASSELLED BOLSTER CUSHION

The embroidery instructions for this project can be found on page 61.

- **You will need** *50 cm (20 in) of furnishing fabric (if a contrasting piping is required, a further 50 cm (20 in) of contrasting fabric must be purchased*
- *piping cord nr 3*
- *bolster cushion pad about 5 cm (2 in) more in length and in circumference than the finished cushion (may have to be made if unavailable commercially)*
- *button thread for hand sewing*

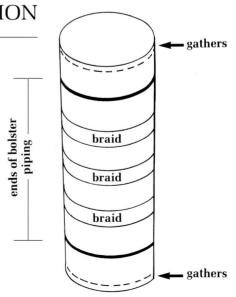

gathers

ends of bolster piping

braid

braid

braid

gathers

Decide on the length of the bolster, the length of braid you have worked will dictate the circumference. Cut panels to make up the length required and machine-stitch them alternatively with the embroidered braid. Stitch a seam along the length of the finished panel, carefully matching the ends of the braids, to make a long tube.

Make a length of piping, at least twice the circumference of the bolster, and attach to each end of the tube. Join the piping as for the plain piped cushion (see page 117). Cut two pieces of fabric equal in length to the circumference of the bolster, and in width to its diameter. Allow for seams on both dimensions. Attach each piece at either end of the tube (see diagram below). Push the bolster cushion pad into the tube so that it sits between the two rows of piping. Run a row of gathers in button thread about 5 cm (2 in) from each end. Pull these gathers up tight and, as you do so, tuck in the raw ends of the fabric on the inside of the cushion. Finish off the ends carefully so that they do not come undone. Make a pair of tassels (see page 115, 2nd paragraph) and attach them where the gathers meet at either end of the bolster.

CURTAIN TIE-BACKS

The embroidery instructions for this project can be found on page 82.

- **You will need** *50 cm (20 in) of light-weight furnishing fabric*
- *a piece of stiffening large enough to line both tie-backs (curtain pelmet interlining is ideal)*
- *four brass rings*

This pattern represents one half of the tie-back. It is reproduced at 50% of its actual size. Enlarge and make yourself a paper pattern. Remember that if the curtains are very full or made of heavy fabric, you should increase the length of the tie-backs by adding fabric along the 'fold' line. If you are not sure, cut a trial piece in calico and try it before you start on the embroidery.

Trim the unstitched canvas edge within 2 cm (2/3 in) of the embroidery. Use the pattern shown opposite to cut pieces of stiffening and lining for each tie-back. Lay the embroidery face down, place the stiffening over it and then the lining. Tack all three layers together along the edge.

Measure the length around the edge of one tie-back. Cut and join enough bias strips (see diagrams 1 and 2, page 117) to bind the edges of both tie-backs.

Begin in the centre of the base of the tie-back and pin the binding – right sides together – all around the edge. Make a neat join and machine this seam. The stitching should be just inside the edge of the embroidery. Trim if necessary and turn the binding over the edge of the tie. Turn in the edge of the bias and slip-stitch on to lining. Attach a brass ring to each end of the tie-back.

brass ring

fold
◄— **add here if greater length is required**

allow for seams

DOORSTOP

The embroidery instructions for this project can be found on page 39.

- **You will need** *a house brick measuring 21.5 x 7.5 x 10 cm (8½ x 3 x 4 in)*
- *a piece of felt for the base*
- *polyester wadding*

Cover up the brick with the wadding. I wrapped it just like a parcel and trimmed off any excess before tacking down the edges.

Trim the unworked canvas edge within 1.5 cm (⅔ in) from the edge of the embroidery. Pin a) and b) right sides together to form the required shape.

Carefully machine or back-stitch these seams by hand so that no unworked canvas shows on the right side. trim the corners. Turn to the right side and insert the padded brick. Fold the unstitched excess canvas over the base of the brick and stitch at the corners. Pin felt base onto the underside of the doorstep and finally, slip-stitch into position.

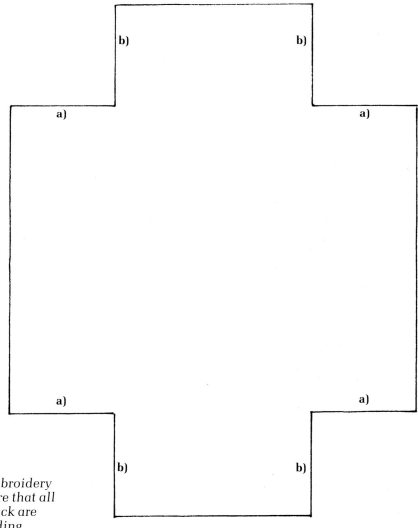

Before mounting the embroidery over the doorstop, ensure that all the hard edges of the brick are fully covered with wadding.

SPECTACLE CASE, CREDIT CARD HOLDER, NEEDLE BOOK, SCISSOR & KEY KEEPERS

The embroidery instructions for the spectacle case and the credit card holder appear on page 71. There are several needle books, *scissor and key keepers featured in this book and they are all made up as explained below. All these small items make handy gifts.*

- **You will need** *a small quantity of the yarn used for the background of the individual object*
- *a piece of felt the same size as the embroidery*
- *a small piece of flannel or felt to make 'pages' for the needle book*

Work a row of long-legged cross stitch (*see* page 110) all the way round the embroidery. This will make an edging and helps turning in the unworked canvas. Trim to within 1.25 cm (½ in) and work a line of herringbone stitches to hold down the raw edges of the canvas – diagram 3), page 117.

The spectacle case. Line with felt as explained above, then fold the embroidery in half and slip-stitch the sides firmly together.

The credit card holder. Line with felt as described above, then fold one third of the embroidery up to form the pocket of the holder. Press down carefully, using a damp cloth. Slip-stitch the edges firmly together, fold the flap down. You might like to add a small press stud or a piece of velcro fastening.

The needle book. Make two 15 cm (6 in) lengths of twisted cord (*see* page 115). Attach one of these ties at each side of the book.

Cut the felt to fit the embroidery exactly and pin together. Slip-stitch around the edge.

Cut two pieces of flannel or felt measuring 4 cm (1.5 in) less than the embroidery in each dimension (use pinking shears if you have them). Fold these 'pages' in half and back-stitch them neatly to the spine of the needle book.

The finished credit card holder

SCISSOR & KEY KEEPERS

- **You will need** *a small quantity of the yarn used for the background*
- *a small quantity of polyester stuffing*

Make a 30 cm (12 in) length of twisted cord (*see page 115*). Trim the canvas to within 1 cm (⅜ in) of the embroidery and fold the edges in. Fold the keeper in half and work a row of long-legged cross stitch (*see page 110*) down the empty threads in the middle. When you reach the corner, carry on with the long-legged cross stitch by taking one canvas thread from each folded-over edge. In other words the embroidery will also form the seam as you work. Fill the keeper with polyester stuffing and tuck in the two ends of the cord to make a loop, before finishing the seam completely.

These tiny cushions can also be filled with lavender to be used as scented bags inside a wardrobe. They can quite literally be made in one evening. This makes them ideal as children's projects. Someone I know has made dozens of these which she uses as decorations on her Christmas tree.

This scissor keeper belongs to The Tudor Collection and you will find the explanations for the embroidery on page 17. The back can be kept plain or, for a more personal gift, can be adorned with a monogram – see page 106.

DRAWSTRING BAG

The embroidery instructions for this project can be found on page 77.

- **You will need** *about 30 cm (12 in) of raw silk or other fabric*
- *a scrap of pelmet stiffening for the base (or a piece of card)*
- *a small quantity of left-over yarn to make twisted cords*

Trim the embroidery within 1.25 cm (½ in) from the edge. Machine or back-stitch the short edges to make a tube. Cut a circle of stiffening and two of fabric, measuring 13 cm (5 in) in diameter (the fabric circles should be a little larger to allow for seams).

Tack the stiffening between the two layers of fabric. Pin the edge of the embroidery, leaving the seam on the outside. You will need to clip the canvas edge carefully to do this. Sew this seam and then bind it with a strip of fabric, by hand or by machine (whatever you feel most comfortable with), taking care not to let any raw canvas show on the outside. To make the top of the bag cut two pieces of fabric 18 x 30 cm (7 x 12 in). Seam these together along the shorter sides. gather the bottom to fit the top edge of the embroidery and pin together, leaving the seams outside, thus no lining is necessary.

Sew this seam and bind it by hand or by machine with a strip of fabric, ensuring that no raw canvas shows.

Turn the top edge of the bag over to make a casing. Make a length of twisted cord of about 60 cm (24 in) – see page 115 – and thread it through the casing.

DRESSING TABLE MAT

The embroidery instructions for this object can be found on page 79.

- **You will need** *a small remnant of silk matching the bag described above*
- *a 10 cm (4 in) square of mounting board (optional)*

Trim the canvas edge within 1.25 cm (½ in). Cut a piece of fabric measuring 80 x 8 cm (32 x 3 in). Seam the ends together to make a continuous loop. Fold it in half lengthwise and run a row of gathers along the raw edges. Pull the threads to fit the edges of the mat. Pin the frill to the mat, carefully spreading the gathers, with the folded edge towards the centre of the mat. Sew this seam carefully so no raw canvas shows around the edge of the mat. Cut a 13 cm (5 in) square of fabric to cover the bottom. If you want to stiffen the base of the mat, tuck the piece of mounting board in as you slip-stitch the square of fabric to the raw side of the embroidery.

EVENING BAG

*The embroidery instructions for this object
can be found on page 95.*

- **You will need** *20 cm (8 in) of silk, satin or moire material*
- *a remnant of similar fabric to make contrasting piping, or
  ready-made satin piping*
- *80 cm (1 yd) of no 2 piping cord*
- *a bag clasp ***

* The clasp I have used was
purchased from an antique
shop. You may need to adapt
the instructions below to fit the
clasp you bought.

The clasp I used is 16 cm (6.25 in) wide and the embroidery panel measures 14 x 10 cm (5.5 x 4 in). I needed about 80 cm (32 in) of piping.

Make a paper pattern based on the sketch below right. The width across the top should be the measurement of the clasp, plus about half as much again to allow for some fullness. To achieve pleasing proportions, the depth of the bag should be about three quarters of the width.

Once you have made your paper pattern, cut three off the shape. One of these pieces will become the back of the bag – the other two will form the lining. Using the paper pattern you then need to work out the width of the side panels which fit with the embroidery to form the front of the bag. (Refer to the photograph of the bag on page 95.) Using the piping foot, sew piping down each side of the embroidery, ensuring that no raw canvas shows on the right side. Attach the side panels. Pipe the outer edge of the bag. Pin the bag front, right sides together, with the back of the bag, and stitch together against the piped edge. Turn right sides out. Stitch the remaining two pieces together to make the

lining. Tuck the lining inside the bag and turn in the top edges. Slip-stitch together. Gather the top to fit the clasp and attach it to the clasp. Old clasps usually have holes along the inner edge to allow for sewing the pocket on to it. If you have purchased a modern clasp, follow the manufacturer's instructions.

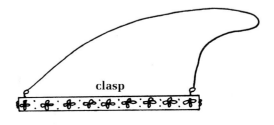

clasp

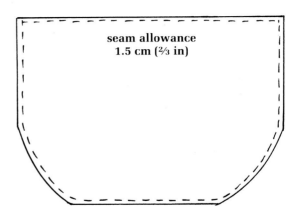

seam allowance
1.5 cm (⅔ in)

LIST OF SUPPLIERS & SERVICES

United Kingdom

Appleton Bros., Thames Works, Church Street, Chiswick, London.
081 994 0711 (Crewel wools.)

DMC Creative World, Pullman Road, Wigston, Leicester. 0533 811040 (Canvas, stranded cotton, Perlé cotton, Médicis wool and general embroidery equipment.) A full list of stockists will be sent on request.

Paterna Yarns, PO Box 1, Ossett, West Yorkshire. 0924 276744 (Paterna Persian yarn.)

The Inglestone Collection, Yells Yard, Cirencester Road, Fairford, Gloucestershire. 0285 712778 (Gold plated needles.)

Framecraft Miniatures, 148–50 High Street, Aston, Birmingham.
021 359 4442 (Trinket box and small silver frames.)

Cleeve Picture Framing, Church Road, Bishops Cleeve, Cheltenham, Gloucestershire. 0242 672785 (Made all the wooden frames shown in this book, including the chessboard).

Roland Bartlett, 2, Beacon Close, Groby, Leicester. 0533 313401 (Made the frame for the fire screen and the large footstool.)

Artisan, High St, Pinner, Middlesex. 081 866 0327.

The Campden Needlecraft Centre, Chipping Campden, Gloucestershire. 0386 840583.

Appleton's Stockists in America and Canada

Handcraft from Europe, PO Box 31524, San Francisco, Ca. 94131-0524.

Louise's Needlework, 45 N. High Street, Dublin, Ohio 43017.

Natalie, 144 N. Larchmont Boulevard, Los Angeles, Ca. 90004.

Needlepoint Inc., 251 Post Street, 2nd Floor, San Francisco, Ca. 94108.

Needle Works Ltd., 4041 Tulane Avenue, New Orleans, La. 70119.

Potpourri Etc., PO Box 78, Redondo Beach, Ca. 90277.

Dick & Jane, 2352 West 41st Avenue, Vancouver, B.C. V6M 2A4.

One Stitch at a Time, PO Box 114, Picton, Ontario K0K 2T0.

Jet Handcraft Studio Ltd, 1847 Marine Drive, West Vancouver, B.C. V7V 1J7.

Appleton's Stockists in Australia and New Zealand

Clifton H. Joseph & Son (Australia) Pty. Ltd, 391–393 Little Lonsdale St., Melbourne, Victoria 3000.

Altamira, 34 Murphy Street, South Yarra, Melbourne, Victoria 3141.

P. L. Stonewall & Co. Pty. Ltd (Flag Division), 52 Erskine Street, Sydney.

Nancy's Embroidery Ltd, 326 Tinakori Road, PO Box 245, Thorndon, Wellington.

Appleton's Stockists in South Africa

Mirza Agency, PO Box 281741, Sunny Side, Pretoria 0132.

Needlepoint, PO Box 662.

Northland 2116, Johannesburg.

Ladylike Den, PO Box 4057, Luipaardsolei 173.

MATERIALS, KITS & MAKING-UP SERVICE

If you have difficulties obtaining supplies in your area, packs of the necessary materials – canvas, yarns and needles – can be supplied. Some of the larger projects can be purchased as kits. A full making-up service of cushions and other objects is also available.
Contact: **Needleworks** by **Sue Hawkins**, The Old School House, Hall Road, Leckhampton, Cheltenham, Gloucestershire. GL53 0HP 0242 584424

INDEX

PICTURE CREDITS

The picture of the seventeenth-century pillow on page 8 is reproduced by kind courtesy of Mallett & Son (Antiques) Ltd; the sixteenth-century Sheldon tapestry on page 88 is reproduced by kind permission of Sudeley Castle, Winchcombe: the antique rug on page 62 by permission of David Black Oriental Carpets, 96 Portland Road, London W11 4LQ.